Hill of Tarvit

Tour of the House

THE NATIONAL TRUST FOR SCOTLAND
5 Charlotte Square Edinburgh EH2 4DU 031-226 5922

Built in 1696 and attributed to Sir William Bruce, the old house on this site was originally called Wemyss Hall. It was a modest building of three bays and two and a half storeys with a central pediment. There are two early photographs of it displayed in the porch. In the 19th century two wings had been added at the back. In 1904 the property was bought by Mr F. B. Sharp, who called in Sir Robert Lorimer to re-build the 1696 house on a much larger scale, in which to display his fine collection of furniture, porcelain and old masters. The date 1906 appears on the Great Hall fireplace.

THE HALL

The tapestries are 16th-century Flemish. The centre of the larger panel is woven with a scene of Alexander the Great after the Battle of Gaugamela receiving the wife and daughters of the defeated king, Darius; Alexander is on a horse and he is flanked by his generals, advisers and retainers; the flower-filled ground is strewn with discarded weapons and booty; the wide borders are designed with small panels depicting figures in landscapes and gardens, classical figures seated, grotesques, arabesques and other typical Renaissance motifs, within architectural surrounds, and flanked by vases of flowers beneath masks and baldequins.

The smaller one is a Flemish Verdure tapestry panel, woven with a hunting party chasing birds, boars and with falconers, the background with a moated château, the wide borders designed with figures making music and conversing in gardens, and with urns of fruit and floral swags.

The furniture is mostly 17th and 18th-century English and Scots oak, but the parquetry bureau is 18th-century Italian. The dwarf cabinet between the main entrance and the Drawing Room door is 16th-century Italian, probably Florentine. Between the windows is a 18th-century Spanish table. The longcase clock is mid 18th-century Flemish, but the movement is English. The large gateleg table and the refectory table are 19th-century; the screen is 18th-century Dutch.

The pictures, starting above the fireplace, are A Landscape with River by David Teniers (Senior) ex Hanham Hall collection; Gentleman in Black with white lace Collar by Jan van Ravensteyn; Little Girl in Red by Jacob Gerritsz Cuyp (1594-1651); a portrait in oils of F. B. Sharp, Esqre, who formed the collections at Hill of Tarvit; and Lady in black dress by Nicholaes Eliasz (1590-1654).

The blue and white porcelain is Chinese, K'ang Hsi (1662-1722). The two black glazed pottery vases are Chinese, Sung dynasty (960-1280). The bronzes are also Chinese.

THE DRAWING ROOM

This room was designed to take Mr Sharp's important collection of French furniture and as such it is a charming pastiche. Much of the plaster decoration and woodwork derive from the styles of 18th-century France.

In accordance with Edwardian taste, the original decoration has been retained, chintz hangings provided, and Oriental rugs laid on the polished floor. The large rug in front of the fireplace is an antique Meshed. The chandelier is of Louis XVI design, made in the late 19th century.

The Louis XV bureau plat in the south window, veneered in kingwood, was made by Jean-Charles Saunier, brother of the more celebrated Charles Saunier. It bears his stamp three times on the underside and some of the ormolu mounts bear a crowned C poinçon. J C. Saunier was made maître ébéniste in 1743.

of this century. The set of chairs is Regency and are of beech grained to simulate rosewood. The small table to the right of the fireplace is a Louis XV guéridon.

The pictures are as follows: over the fireplace a Waterway with Shipping by Jan van Beecq; on each side of the south window are two George III silkwork panels; the silhouettes date from the Regency period. On the west wall over the secrétaire is a small oil sketch of Hampstead Heath, ascribed to John Constable. The remaining painting is by Salomon Ruisdale.

The decorative porcelain is mostly Chinese Ch'ien Lung.

THE DRESSING ROOM

Like the bedroom, this room has been redecorated as closely to the original as possible. The secrétaire to the right of the window is Dutch neo-classical, the armoire on the east wall is French and dates from the early years of the reign of Louis XVI. It is veneered with panels of kingwood à quatre faces and the whole is enriched with ormolu borders and mounts. To the left of the fireplace stands a satinwood bonheur du jour. The bed in the Chinese taste is contemporary with the house.

The pictures are as follows: over the bedside table a small study of Gipsies round a fire, by George Morland; to the left of the fireplace, a picture by Hendrik Dubbels; the important painting over the fireplace is by Abraham Beerstraten. The remaining pictures are Dutch 17th-century depicting winter scenes and are unascribed.

The decorative china here as in the bedroom is mostly 18th-century Chinese.

The other important signed piece of furniture is the mahogany commode with a Siena marble top on the west wall. It dates from the reign of Louis XVI and bears the signature of Adam Weisweiler. Born at Neuwied on the Rhine c. 1750 where he studied in the workshop of David Roentgen, Weisweiler was established as an 'artisan-libre' about the beginning of the reign of Louis XVI and before 1777. He was made Mâitre in 1778, and was living in the Rue Sainte Antoine. He seems to have worked for the Marchand Entrepreneur, D. Daguerre, and supplied furniture for the Royal Palaces, especially Saint-Cloud. He worked throughout the Revolution and Empire and received commissions from Queen Hortense.

In the west window embrasure there is a small Transitional secrétaire à abattant veneered with kingwood panels à quatre faces, dating from the last years of the reign of Louis XV, circa 1770-1774. A somewhat larger secrétaire of the same period, veneered with marquetry and tulipwood and with a Brescia marble top, stands to the right of the fireplace; to the left is a 19th-century commode of drum shape, also with a Brescia marble top.

The suite de salon comprising four fauteuils and one canapé is Louis XVI, in the style of Jacob; it is covered in Beauvais tapestry. The single giltwood fauteuil is of Louis XVI design and the four boudoir chairs of Louis XV design. Another copy of the same date in the style of Louis XVI is the small guéridon made by the firm of Edwards and Roberts of Wardour Street, London. The circular satinwood inlaid teatable is Dutch, and dates from c. 1790; a similar one is illustrated in the Dictionary of English Furniture. The mahogany commode with the white marble top on the north wall is Louis XVI. The three stools are English and date from the early years of the last century.

The pictures, starting over the door and working in a clockwise direction, are as follows: Still Life by Gordon Shields; pastel portrait of Mrs Sharp drawn in Florence in 1904 by J. Rolshoven; underneath, a small 18th-century English landscape; a pastel portrait of Mr Hugh Sharp drawn in Florence in 1904; pastel portrait of Miss Stewart of Ardvorlich by Allan Ramsay (1713-1784); Still Life by A. D. Muir (over door); Les Violettes and Les Giroflees by Henri Fantin-Latour (1836-1904); Dutch 17th-century skating scene; and an imaginary seaport with classical buildings by Abraham Storck.

On the north wall there is a Skating Scene after Van der Neer; a Frozen River Scene with Figures, by Klaes Molenar; Winter Landscape with Frozen River by Brueghel; Winter Landscape by Adriken Van der Velde; and a pair of Seascapes by Samuel Scott.

The plates on the wall with predominately green decoration are Famille Verte and date from the early 18th century, K'ang Hsi. The Buddhistic lions, vases and seated goddesses are blanc de Chine, late 17th-century. The porcelain with pink floral decoration (Famille Rose) is later, Chien Lung (1736-1795).

THE LIBRARY

Most of the furniture dates from the reign of George III — the side chairs reflecting the designs of Thomas Chippendale, and the satinwood tables those of Sheraton. The sofa table in the centre of the room is Regency and the pole screens are Victorian.

The pictures, starting behind the door and working round the room in a clockwise direction, are as follows: Mrs Tyndall Bruce of Falkland, by Sir Henry Raeburn (1756-1823); a portrait of Mrs Brown and Miss E. Brown, wife and daughter of Robert Brown of Newhall, by Sir J. Watson Gordon; John Tait of Harvieston by Sir Henry Raeburn; a Flower Piece by Henri Fantin-Latour (1836-1904); Winter Landscape by George Morland (1763-1804); Still Life by Abraham van Beyeren (1620-1691); maritime piece by Albert Cuyp (1620-1690); Mrs Young, sister of Charles James Fox, by Allan Ramsay (1713-1784); Lady in a Blue Dress, by Allan Ramsay; Mrs Muir of Caldwell, by Allan Ramsay; Captain Thomas Wallace, by Allan Ramsay.

The blue and white porcelain is Chinese and dates mostly from the K'ang Hsi dynasty (1662-1722). The bronzes are also Chinese.

THE DINING ROOM

The dining room table is Regency, and was made to a design by Gillows of Lancaster who patented this model for 'Imperial Dining Tables' early in the 19th century. The harlequin set of chairs are Chippendale, likewise the serving table between the doors and the four-tier dumb waiter. The sideboard between the windows is late 18th-century Scottish, with its typical raised shelf at the back. The sarcophagus under the serving table is a Regency cellarette. The bracket clock is a mid-Georgian example in a Chinese Chippendale case The wine cooler in the south window is Brescia marble and the carpet is Sparta.

Starting behind the door, the pictures are: Peacocks, Cockatoos, etc., by Francis Barlow (17th-century); Peg Woffington by Joseph Highmore (1692-1780); portrait of a lady by Paulus Moreelse (1571-1638); Still Life by Willem Heda (1593-1680); portrait of a lady in a black and red dress with a white ruff, dated 1659, by Cornelius Janssens (1593-1661)

The porcelain and bronzes are Chinese. The bronze seated figure of Buddha is Siamese, 17th-century. The porcelain on the chimney piece is K'ang Hsi; the pair of pear shaped vases with deer mask handles on the window sills are 19th-century Chinese.

The silver galleon is a 19th-century German Nef. The silver on the dumb waiter and sideboard is mostly Georgian, although the silver models of animals are German but have British import marks.

THE DINING ROOM PASSAGE

The furniture continues in the same idiom as that in the Hall. It is mostly oak. The chest on stand under the window is Jacobean, the dresser mid-Georgian. The armchairs are 17th-century, English. The pair of walnut chairs on the south wall covered in Cordova leather are 17th-century Spanish, and the miniature cabinet is mid 18th-century Dutch.

The pictures on the north wall (dresser wall) consist of a pair of 17th-century Venetian landscapes and, between them, a Still Life by J. S. Noble. Opposite hang a pair of Still Lifes by Jakob Bogdani, between which is another by an unknown Dutch 17th-century artist.

The porcelain is Chinese, but the six plates with the centres decorated with flower heads, on the dresser, and the punch bowl are English tin-glazed earthenware, and the tobacco jar is Delft.

THE SMOKING ROOM

The original name has been retained but the room has been furnished with items from the Sharp collection as an additional sitting room; at one time it also contained a billiard table.

The important writing desk across the corner is French, Louis XVI; strictly speaking it is a bureau-plât bonheur du jour, in the Style Etrusque. The tall chest of drawers to the left of the west window is also French, likewise in the Etruscan style, but dating from the early years of the 19th century. The pair of occasional tables at each end of the sofa are English Regency; they are of satinwood, cross-banded with coromandel wood. The side chairs reflect the designs of Thomas Chippendale and the satinwood sofa table dates from the closing years of the 18th century. The case containing a collection of Japanese bronzes started life as a barrel organ and is typical of the conversions that were made in the early years of this century. The bronze model of a duck is 18th-century, Chinese. The wrought iron standard lamps are of typical Edwardian design, and the shades are in the style that would have been fashionable at the beginning of the century. The large circular porcelain dishes are Japanese Imari dating from the end of the 17th century, and the blue and white vases are Chinese of similar date.

The still life painting to the left of the bookcase is by de Heem (1606-84); that on the right is quite a well-known subject — 'the Blackheath Golfers' — originally painted by Abott (1760-1803). The painting over the writing desk is by Hendrik Avercamp (1585-1634). The still life on the south wall, featuring a crab, a peeled lemon and a blue and white dish, is by Pieter Claesz, and the other still life, over the fireplace, is by Hendrick van Zuylen.

The carpet is a Donegal.

THE GALLERY

Originally the Gallery stretched from one end of the house to the other, but now it is only half its original size. The great cabinet on the south wall was made at the beginning of the century in the Chinese Chippendale taste. It contains a collection of Chinese porcelain, mostly dating from the middle of the 18th century. Opposite stands a 17th-century Italian walnut cassone, on top of which is a miniature cassone of similar provenance and date. On each side is a pair of Chinese cloisonné vases. The suite of chairs in simulated bamboo disposed along the gallery dates from the last quarter of the 18th century, and is made in the Chinese Chippendale style. The ship-model is a sail and steam frigate of circa 1850. Frigates were small fast warships carrying their main armament on the lower-deck. Due to their speed one of their chief functions was to keep ahead of the fleet, seek out the enemy and act as communications link. This particular model illustrates the period when steam power was beginning to vie with sail power for superiority. The early propellers were twin bladed and were fitted so that they could be hauled up into the hull. This was to prevent drag when the vessel was proceeding under sail. At the same time the telescopic funnel and steam pipes could be wound down. This elaborate procedure caused the expression 'up funnel, down screw' to be used when proceeding under steam. Full sailing rig continued to be used for warships until the 1870s.

The pictures are as follows: on the staircase the two large paintings of dead game birds are by Jan Weenix; the one depicting fighting cocks etc. is by Melchior Hondecoeter. On the south wall, halfway along, is a delightful painting by Francis Wheatley entitled 'The Love Letter', and at the west end on each side two paintings by J. F. Herring, Senior. On the north wall hangs a landscape with a hawking party by Philips Wouwerman.

THE SOUTH WEST BEDROOM

This was probably the principal bedroom on account of its delightful position. It has a dressing room next door and an entrance lobby containing well fitted cupboards and wardrobes.

The fireplace dates from 1905. As many as possible of the original electrical fittings, with the exception of the chandelier, have been retained. The wallpaper is almost identical with the one that was originally used. There was no record of the former carpet, but the one laid was specially made and it conforms in size to the original one. The trellis pattern of the glazed chintz is a design much used throughout the house.

The secrétaire in the south west corner is Dutch, in the neo-classical taste, and dates from the last quarter of the 18th century. The chest of drawers just inside the door dates from the 1750s; the miniature chest on top, of similar design, is an apprentice piece. Above hangs an 18th-century Venetian looking-glass. In accordance with Edwardian practice, a sofa table has been used as a dressing table. The beds and bedside tables all date from the beginning

Insight
Holland

Insight Holland

MAX DENDERMONDE

KOSMOS UTRECHT ANTWERP

N O O R D Z E E
(NORTH SEA)

Rottum
Schiermonnikoog
Ameland
Terschelling
GRONINGEN
Vlieland
Leeuwarden
Groningen
Texel
FRIESLAND
Assen
WADDENZEE
DRENTE
IJsselmeer
Noordoost-
polder
NOORD-
Alkmaar
Hoorn
Zwolle
HOLLAND
Lelystad
OVERIJSSEL
Flevopolder
Almelo
Haarlem
Hen
Amsterdam
Almere
Deventer
Gooi
Apeldoorn
Enschede
Amersfoort
GELDERLAND
Leiden
Veluwe
UTRECHT
Den Haag
ZUID-
Utrecht
Arnhem
(The Hague)
Delft
Gouda
Achterhoek
Lek
Rijn
Schiedam
Rotterdam
(Rhine)
HOLLAND
Waal
Nijmegen
Dordrecht
Maas
Duisburg
s-Hertogenbosch
NOORD-BRABANT
Breda
Tilburg
Eindhoven
Düsseldorf
Middelburg
ZEELAND
Neuss
LIMBURG
Brugge
Antwerpen
(Bruges)
(Antwerp)
Ke
Gent
(Co
(Ghent)
Heerlen
Maastricht
Duinkerken
Brussel
Aken
(Dunkirk)
(Brussels)
Schelde
Roubaix
(Scheldt)
Luik
Lille
(Liège)
BELGIË
Lens
(BELGIUM)
Charleroi
FRANKRIJK
(FRANCE)
Sambre
Maas
LUX.

ENGELAND
(ENGLAND)
Great Yarmouth
Harwich
Dover

WEST-DUITSLAND
(WEST-GERMA...

0   50   100 km

Contents

The book came about as the result of an initiative of
Wereldcontact.

Europe on a small scale

Insight Holland

'If you want to get to know the Netherlands, go stand on a chair and you will be able to see all of it.'

That the Netherlands would appear to be almost impossible to find on a world map is in sharp contradiction to the country's glorious history, as well as its role in the world economy today. For western Europe in particular the Netherlands is – not least because of its geographical situation – an important, even an essential country.

For this reason it is not in fact so difficult to find, in spite of its small size. First seek out Great Britain on the map. To the east, across the waters of the North Sea, lies another large country, West Germany. That small patch wedged in between Germany and the North Sea is all there is to the Netherlands. The country is also referred to as Holland, sometimes the Low Countries, and very occasionally, as the land of Rembrandt. But the official name is the Netherlands. Even so, a great many people prefer Holland, a name often used with affection.

A close look at the map reveals that a number of major European rivers find their outlets to the North Sea in the Netherlands. The largest and best-known of these is the Rhine, which begins in Switzerland and flows through Germany, where it is not only responsible for those picturesque landscapes, but also plays a vital role in the economy, not to mention art and culture. The second major river is the Maas, or Meuss, which flows from France through Belgium, entering the Netherlands near the town of Maastricht shortly after passing through the important Belgian industrial city of Liège. The third river is the Scheldt, which also flows through Belgium after originating in France, and which has been an important source of the prosperity of the Belgian port city, Antwerp. These three European rivers form together a delta, which has led to the comment that a great part of the Netherlands is made up of the dregs of Europe. Originally this marshy area, half water and half land, was hardly habitable. Indications of this can still be found in the southwest of the Netherlands, where large parcels of land were until recently still genuine islands, and where one of the eleven Dutch provinces is called Zeeland ('sea land'). Until well into the 1980s, the Netherlands was occupied here with improving the defenses against the raw North Sea, while at the same time giving the region a highly distinctive look of its own. That is, if you didn't already happen to know it, a peculiarly Dutch characteristic: reshaping the geography of their own country. The Dutch have in fact created a large part of their land themselves. This alone is already sufficient in itself to make the Netherlands one of the most enthralling countries in the world. Keeping their land dry is a ceaseless task that occupies all of the Dutch together. Dry feet take precedence over full stomachs in the national well-being, although the Dutch individually are not preoccupied with this every minute of the day. It does partially explain the alertness of this small population, however, its resolute approach to the sciences, the vigilant entrepreneurial passion for commerce, industry and agriculture.

The first thing likely to strike visitors arriving at Amsterdam's Schiphol international airport – one of the most important in Europe – after they have been efficiently helped to their baggage and through customs and have settled themselves into their bus seat, taxicab or train compartment, is the manner in which the traffic, roadways, the system of traffic signs and the cohesion of dikes, viaducts, canals and bridges, are organized. Without such a smooth, perfectly meshing organization, this small, low and over-populated country could not survive.

Upon arrival in a city, though, Amsterdam for example, one is likely to be much more struck by the way in which all road users seem to go their own individual way and apparently do pretty much whatever they please. All stand firmly on their rights and will go to any lengths to prove it. Perplexed observers have written extensively about this but it still goes on, year in and year out. 'Manners! In Amsterdam they've apparently never heard of them!' writes one English journalist. 'Pushing, shoving, jogging make up the normal demeanor of Amsterdammers and this universal behavior seems to go back as far as Amsterdam itself. Not only are you confronted with a lack of ordinary, everyday decency as you walk along the streets, but the manners of the drivers, cyclists and all the rest are also clearly of a sort that can only be found in Amsterdam.' And in the rest of the Netherlands, we would add. But also this: it is not as bad as it seems. And it also forms part of the great Dutch paradox, which combines a strong

In 1934 KLM took part in the London-Melbourne air race with the DC-2 'Uiver', the only participant with passengers on board. To commemorate that legendary flight of 50 years ago KLM repeated it at a somewhat slower tempo, again with a DC-2, in the winter of 1983-84.

sense of individualism with an equally strong sense of community. Both are explained by students of the national character as arising from the equally paradoxical nature of the land itself: fertile land, that in fact should belong to the domain of the sea. On the one hand, the Dutch have always had to struggle to wrest that land from the sea, while on the other, the sea has meant for them, as voyagers and fishers, their freedom, an independance that placed them above the rule of law – according to one of the explanations, anyway.

Insisting on their rights while at the same time tolerant, magnanimous and generous, that is the Dutch national character. When in 1953 the southwest of the Netherlands experienced its last – so far – great flood disaster, with more than 1800 lives lost and many thousands of people deprived of all their worldly possessions, the entire country sprang forth in testimony to its sense of

Schiphol, the major international airport of the Netherlands. Five to ten flights depart here daily for America and Canada alone.

9

*Characteristic for the low farmland, a
ditch to carry the water off.*

*The flooded Tielerwaard, along the Waal.
A regularly occurring danger: the water.*

community spirit, with voluntary collections – the equivalent of many millions of dollars – with clothing and household goods, but also with more direct aid: thousands of Dutch citizens abandoned hearth and home to help with the evacuation of the stricken population and the plugging of the breached dikes. As a result of the disaster, new, far-reaching legislation was quickly brought into being by Parliament, which led to the development of an expensive, prolonged, but conclusive protection scheme for the southwest Netherlands and other parts of the country: the Delta plan. This envisioned, among other things, a drastic shortening of the Netherlands' long and vulnerable coastline. This more than 600 miles of dangerous coast also demonstrates another Dutch paradox, however, since large sections include the most beautiful and popular beaches of western Europe. During the summer they are more overpopulated, with Germans, the French, Belgians and

10

In spite of the many good facilities that have been created for cyclists, difficult situations still occur. The cyclist has rights and obligations defined by law. In that respect he is the equal of the motorist in the Netherlands.

Just imagine: with a population of about 14 million people there are 10 to 11 million bicycles. This means that many people possess two bicycles: one for riding to work and one as touring bike.

the English, than is the country itself.

How small is the Netherlands exactly? A joker once said: 'If you want to get to know the Netherlands, go stand on a chair and you will be able to see all of it.' That is almost true. From east to west it is not more than 105 miles wide. (It still took Hitler's troops five days to cover in May, 1940; the peace-loving, poorly-armed Dutch fought like inexperienced lions for their centuries-old freedom.) From the southernmost point, near Maastricht, to the northernmost island of Rottum is 190 miles as the plane flies. A modern jet can do it, via the beautifully reconstructed town of Arnhem ('A Bridge Too Far') in about 15 minutes. The head of state, since 1898 always a queen, of whom Beatrix is the third, can spend every evening at home regardless of which out of the way town she has visited that day. It is a small land, thus, on the order of Belgium, Denmark or Switzerland.

More than fourteen million people live in this small, vulnerable land, one of the most densely populated in the world. There are well over 1,000 people per square mile on average. They are in fact rather unevenly distributed over the Dutch landscape.

Years ago the government tabled ambitious plans to achieve a reasonable population distribution over the entire country, and to give all cities and regions equal opportunities as far as possible. But these ideas had to be abandoned as the greatest concentration was traditionally bound to a few western cities in a virtually completely urbanized area where 47% of the total population lives. This area is known collectively as the *Randstad*, or 'rim city'. The largest cities whithin it are Amsterdam, Rotterdam and The Hague, each with a greater population that hovers around the one million level.

This Randstad makes up one of the largest metropolitan centers of Europe. Here, at the mouths of the European rivers on the North Sea, between Paris, Londen, Hamburg and the Ruhr, enormous economic interests are concentrated, leading centers of trade, major ports and important industries are located, and here, too, lies Schiphol, that all-important airport. In the last 20 years it has stimulated a new urbanization and industrialization of its immediate environs.

In theory, all those fourteen million Dutch citizens have the same obligations, such as compulsory national service, and the same rights. At specified times fully democratic elections are held on three levels: municipal, provincial and national. These are proportional elections, in which each vote carries the same weight. If a party secures 10% of the vote, then it receives 10% of the total seats. For elections to the lower house (150 members, the largest body in Parliament), the entire country forms a single constituency. These elections are held every four years. Members of the upper house (75) are not directly elected, but indirectly, once in four years, by the members of the eleven Provincial States. This last collective body is in turn directly elected by residents of the individual provinces.

The government is not seated in Amsterdam, the official capital, but in The Hague, the royal 'residency' formally known by its stately name of *'s-Gravenhage*, the country estate of the Count of Holland. The business of government is still conducted from a complex of partly medieval buildings known as the Binnenhof (Inner Court), which can be viewed. Parliamentary debares can also be followed from the public tribunes.

In the court capital is also housed another large organization, which is sometimes referred to as the 'state within the state': Rijkswaterstaat, or the government department of public works. This is responsible for keeping the country dry, maintaining the dikes, canals, roads and the like, and for the design and commission of major new public works. If the entire complex of dikes in the Netherlands – the result of centuries and centuries of labor – can already legitimately be regarded as the eighth wonder of the world, then the last great engineering project of the Delta plan is certainly that wonder's shining, stunning, crowning symbol of all the ingenuity, daring and spirit of self-sacrifice that make up the Dutch character. This is a variable dam in the Oosterschelde, one of the huge estuaries protected from the sea by the project. Originally it had been intended to cut the vulnerable estuary completely off from the sea with an 'ordinary' dike, which would have meant the eventual desalination and destruction of the ecologically rich salt-water area. In the early 1970s this plan began to arouse the opposition of all manner of interested groups. They got their way. The estuary would retain its life-giving link with the sea through a half-open dam, that would have to be fully closable during storms and times of high water. And so it was constructed. It was a fantastic undertaking, the largest and most complicated engineering project of its kind ever attempted in the Netherlands, or the entire world for that matter. An American, visiting the construction site like so many thousands of others, asked: 'What big company would take on that kind of financing risk? And what kind of return do they expect from it?' He was told that the Dutch State was paying the bill and that no direct profit could be expected. 'So,' said the American after lengthy consideration, 'the taxpayer is the shareholder in this dream?' And that had to be acknowledged, for the Latin motto in Zeeland's heraldic crest, *Luctor et emergo* ('I struggle and emerge') – one pictures the Dutch lion cutting through the waves — is in fact

The Lower House of Parliament meets, at the Binnenhof in The Hague. The Dutch Parliament consists of an Upper House (75 members) and a Lower House, which is the most important political body and of which the 150 representatives are directly chosen in general elections.

the motto of the entire nation.

There are certainly some in the Netherlands who feel that this intricate, money-burning technical display is going too far, but for most pride wins out over the knowledge that they are having to pay for it all. Aside from that is the feeling that if Rijkswaterstaat is for it, then it must be a good thing. While this institution is not quite sacred, it does enjoy the utmost confidence. Even the Germans who took over the country between 1940 and 1945 preferred not to tamper with it too much; it was all too complicated for them. The Napoleonic occupiers at the beginning of the nineteenth century also left the dikes and polders to the public works people. To go back even farther: even the Spanish occupiers at the end of the sixteenth century had to partially give up the power struggle over the Netherlands when the Dutch brought water into the battle by choosing to inundate entire regions. Against that the Spanish were helpless.

That battle against Spanish domination was what actually forged the Netherlands into a single nation, as we shall see further on in this book. Later generations found it difficult to comprehend the fierceness of that struggle, for the love of peace was for a long time stronger than any willingness to fight. But during the emergence of the labor movement at the end of the nineteenth century the old fighting spirit also re-emerged. In 1903 the first great strikes broke out among the railway workers. After that mass demonstrations became the order of the day. During the first world war the Netherlands remained neutral and the entire population was more firmly anti-war than ever. Also after the war ended, in the 1920s, there were even mass demonstrations against armament. In 1940, when the Germans invaded, the Dutch were thus far from adequately prepared. The resistance against the occupiers only gradually gained force, but it was fierce in later years. This war against the nazis marks a turning point for the Netherlands. After 1945 the nation discovered a new common vitality; the land acquired a modern structure. Within a short period many major changes took place. What had been a land of seafarers, farmers and merchants became a nation of workers, teachers, and later, of civil servants and other public service employees, and finally, of large and small technocrats. Together with all of the Western economies, the Netherlands became caught up in an accelerating current that has since again subsided into a more sluggish stream in the 1980s. The tide appears to be turning anew.

In principle, the Netherlands can draw upon a total work force of five million men and women. In these times of structural change not all can find work, but everyone is still provided for: the Netherlands has become a welfare state, and no one has to beg.

Construction of the pillars for the closable dam in the Eastern Scheldt between Noord Beveland and Schouwen Duiveland.

13

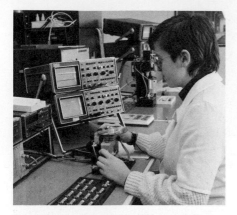

Work in the electronics industry: adjustment and control of the light pen for the Compact Disc.

Queen Beatrix (31-1-1938) entered into marriage on March 10th, 1966, with Claus von Amsberg. They have had three sons: Willem Alexander (27-4-1967), Johan Friso (25-9-1968) and Constantijn Christof (11-10-1969).

The worth of each individual, well-off or close to the poverty line, is highly held in this nation. Thirty-two percent of the working population is employed in industry, for a large part in the chemical industry. Only six percent is directly employed in agriculture and the fishing industry, although the economic share of these sectors is very much greater. Both have a very high level of productivity. It is not surprising, in this land of port industries and large transport companies, that no less than 47% works in the service sector.

Those out of work continued to increase in number in 1983 and 1984. Many were young people. This is inevitable, for out of every hundred Dutch persons, forty are under the age of 30. It is largely these – frequently unemployed – youths who are quick to seize any opportunity to rock the public boat, usually in the form of protest demonstrations – of which not a few are aimed at obtaining a place to live.

In principle everyone who is unable or unwilling to buy a home has the right to a rental dwelling, but there are not enough to go around. The urgent housing shortage after World War Two might have been solved had the structure of society not changed: smaller families and more single person households, not only through divorce but also from free choice. A comfortable home where one can relax with pleasure, the intimacy of home life – this is quintessentially Dutch. In the past more than now the curtains of windows facing into the street were left open. Could this be because the home is regarded as a form of communication, a mode of expression? Some interpret it more in terms of the Dutch preference for openness.

Certainly openness is regarded practically as an ideology. In Dutch literature only the 'confessional' first person form can really achieve widespread appreciation. In journalism, in interviews, the tone is usually severe: the interviewer should preferably leave his victim looking foolish and exposed. The hard interview is almost a national folk sport. This has its positive side: the Netherlands is a country with little corruption. Shades of wrong-doing are also not tolerated. No one is spared, not even a member of the royal family. 'Tall trees catch much wind' is a frequently-heard Dutch saying.

The Netherlands is full of paradoxes. Amsterdam, the official capital, has been regarded as an anti-monarchial 'republican' city for centuries. Residents of other big cities might also be termed republican, especially if they also happen to harbor left-wing sentiments, as more than thirty percent to nearly forty percent of the electorate invariably does. Approximately the same share of the population is Christian democrat. Up to a quarter votes for the

Wilhelmina, queen of the Netherlands from 1898 to 1948. She was married to Duke Hendrik van Mecklenburg-Schwering. From the marriage Juliana was born.

Juliana, queen from 1948 to 1980, with her husband Bernard, prince of Lippe-Biesterveld. They have four daughters, Beatrix (1938), Irene (1939), Margriet (1943) and Christina (1947). The family mainly resided at the royal palace at Soestdijk.

free-enterprise liberals (conservatives in Dutch politics). The influence of the communists is negligible.

The Netherlands became a formal monarchy under the House of Orange only in 1814, after the Napoleonic period. Even so, the royal connection goes back to the very founding of the nation: the Father of the fatherland was Prince William of Orange (1533-1584). The first Dutch queen, Wilhelmina, who succeeded to the throne in 1898, is a descendant of his. She made the monarchy popular to broad sections of the population during the second world war by her militant stance in leading the resistance as head of the government in exile in London. Her daughter, Juliana, has also been a much-loved monarch. Much that is good can be said of her, not least that she has perfectly prepared her own eldest daughter for wearing the crown. These are very old-fashioned words for a monarch such as Queen Beatrix of Orange, who is a good-humored, vivacious and erudite woman, the best representation that a country could wish for. Some republicans now say that if the country ever does opt for a president, it should be Beatrix. When she took up her task in 1980, Queen Beatrix stated: 'In a free and pluriform community such as ours, it is unavoidable that differences will arise and find expression. It is essential to the resolution of these that the opponent be seen not as an enemy, but as someone with a different opinion.'

The center of
the world

Insight Holland

In the Netherlands history is almost a living thing: you encounter it around every corner.

The more than fourteen million Dutch live, as it were, on a day-to-day basis with their common history, even if they are not consciously aware of this every minute of the day. Still, they are immersed in it; history is more than dry facts out of a book. To take an extreme example, we can imagine ourselves in the capital, on Dam Square. This is the place where Amster*dam* came into existence when the river Amstel was dammed to cut it off from the dangerous Zuiderzee ('Southern Sea'), or to be more precise, from the inlet of the sea known as the IJ. That already says much: history and hydraulic engineering are closely intertwined in the 'Low Countries.'

We are standing thus in the middle of 'the Dam', facing to the northwest. Turning first to the left we see the Dam Palace. This is now a royal palace, but originally it was just the Amsterdam town hall, as indicated by the name of the street starting from the other side, the Raadhuisstraat. This massive, imposing structure was designed by a famous builder of the seventeenth century, Jacob van Campen. It is a splendid monument to monied vanity, for in that time the rich made the laws. Only the votes of the wealthy counted, and a small upper crust ran things as they saw fit. It would be a long time yet before the Netherlands would become a genuine democracy, with the right to vote for all, rich and poor, man and woman. But the basis for that democracy was laid in the opulent seventeenth century. The Dam Palace is an example of baroque architecture and a symbol of affluence and bourgeois self-esteem. It was completed in the middle of that mighty century, around 1655.

The building to the right of it, known as the New Church, is much older yet. It dates from before the Reformation and was thus orig-

17

inally catholic, just as everything and everyone else in the western world; all of life was saturated with Rome, and with the power centered there. Construction of the New Church was begun in 1414, a time when Amsterdam had already expanded to the point of requiring a second parish. Thus the name 'New' Church. It is a lovely example of late gothic architecture. Much cost and effort have gone into its recent restoration.

If we now look again in our original direction, down the wide boulevard of the Damrak, we find at the end the Central Station, the most imposing railway station building in the Netherlands. It was erected in the last quarter of the nineteenth century. The architects P.J.H. Cuypers and A.L. van Gendt designed this 'baroque' building in the 'Dutch Renaissance' style, as was done with many important buildings in that time. The Central Station was completed in 1889. With the construction of this building Amsterdam's natural inlet from the Southern Sea was cut off.

We shift our gaze now to the right side of the Dam and find it captured by a somewhat dark, harsh building, that was completed only four years later. It was designed by the important Dutchman Hendrik Petrus Berlage (1856-1934), who had a much more rational style that contained characteristics of what would later become known as the 'New Sobriety'. Berlage also wrote on many subjects, including 'Aesthetics and Society'. And by society he meant the total society, thus all classes of the population, including the working class. It was in this period that weekly publications such as 'Justice for All' appeared, and that demands for universal suffrage began to be heard. It is thus a nice coincidence for historians that Berlage's Bourse, or stock exchange – for that is the name of that dark building – was completed in 1903, the year that the Netherlands saw national strikes for the first time, by the railway workers, who for once demonstrated their power. It achieved disappointingly little at the time, but fourteen years later, in 1917, all men were granted the right to vote and five years later women were also allowed to participate in the democratic process.

At the corner of the Damrak and the Dam stands the Bijenkorf, a giant of the age of 'les grands magasins', the great department stores. For more than half a century it has stamped Amsterdam with the image of a city where everything was for sale. Architecturally there is little to be said about it: it radiates a sort of middle-class solidness; come on in, this is your place, too. Its history – from a rather exclusive establishment to a store dealing in luxury goods for the masses – is symbolic of the development of the consumer society. In addition, this firm also fulfils a cultural function with 'theme' weeks devoted to different countries and with literary markets.

The Dam with the Royal Palace, the centerpiece of Amsterdam. The palace dates from the Golden (17th) century, designed by architect Jacob van Campen.

Amsterdam

Returning to the middle of Dam Square, we come to the so-called Dam Monument, a bare, stark, upthrusting pillar. It was designed by architect Jacobus Johannes Pieter Oud, founder of the artistic school De Stijl, and by the sculptor John Raedecker. This memorial to the victims of the second world war, who are still commemorated here every fourth of May, was completed in 1949. It is an odd, in fact an ugly monument that was the butt of all kinds of remarks and jokes in its first years. Were then designers perhaps attempting, through the adoption of this harshly simple form, to escape from the complexities of their own time, from the somber uncertainties of the cold war era? For that was when it was built, after all. The monument manages to be a monument without being monumental in substance. At the same time, a remarkable development has taken place around this monument, for it has risen above its original purpose as a tragic reminder to become a carefree symbol of a new kind of personal and individual freedom, particularly for the young. On a typical summer day the foot of the stone pillar as well as the surrounding terraces will be covered with hundreds of young people from dozens of countries, playing guitar, talking, loafing or waiting – maybe for days – for a friend from a distant place. The monument has acquired the function of an international meeting point, a free and open center of social intercourse. Certainly it is a center of personal freedom, and that is how the modern Dutch experience it; having known real oppression they keenly appreciate the freedom they now enjoy, and partly for that reason they feel a sense of personal responsibility for what is happening in other parts of the world. Nowhere is there so much involvement in the developing countries of the Third World, or for that matter in the entire world. And nowhere are people of all persuasions so ready to turn out for public demonstrations in support of humanitarian causes everywhere. And here we have managed, without taking a single step from our original starting place, to visually make our way from the early power of the catholic church and then that of the wealthy merchants, through the rise of industry and the evolution of society to a new affluence and freedom for all. Nearly six centuries of history.

Amsterdam is by no means the only place where this six centuries of history can be virtually taken in at a glance. In practically all of the older Dutch towns – and there are certainly enough of those – a spot can be found where monuments from many centuries tell their silent tales. The best guide to these hidden corners is the local VVV (tourist office). Stand, gaze, and be captivated by the riches. It is also possible, of course, to take a different kind of trip through Holland's living history by traveling extensively through the country itself. A good place to start is in the northeastern

The Tuschinski Theater in Amsterdam, which the film theater operator Abram Icek Tuschinski had built in 1921. A classic example of a movie house in the 1920s.

19

Archeological research at a hunnebed, once a communal burial vault of the new stone age built there about 3000 b.c. near the village of Drouwen in Drenthe.

province of Drenthe, which is littered with impressive megalithic tombs known as 'hunnebeds', left behind by a people who inhabited this region three thousand years before the birth of Christ. Something is also known of even earlier times, but that is going back to the misty past of the earliest prehistory. With the arrival of the Romans, not long before the birth of Christ, the picture becomes clearer. In Maastricht history can be literally touched; during the many excavations such artifacts as a Roman relief of the god Apollo have been found. This places us between the first and fourth century A.D. From the time of Charlemagne – 768-814 – we can still find remnants of his residence in Nijmegen, dating from the ninth century. From the period of romanesque architecture – from the 10th to the 13th century – many examples can be found in the Netherlands. We choose the lovely church of the former abbey of Rolduc, near Kerkrade, and the 'Dom' in

The gothic church St. Bavo in Haarlem.

The famed St. Bavo church in Haarlem dates from as long ago as the 14th century, the period in which the town grew into a community of considerable aspect. The edifice is a late gothic cross church. The church has undergone several restorations, particularly since 1876. The famous organ dates from 1738, and was built by Christian Müller. The choir benches and the choir railing date from the beginning of the seventeenth century.

Utrecht, which was completed in 1382 after more than sixty years of labor. Then we make a leap from the crossed to the pointed arch – from romanesque to gothic. There is also plenty of choice here and we take – at random – the church of Saint Bavo in Haarlem. There are many beautiful gothic towers in the Netherlands. It should not be forgotten that all of the money required for such constructions had to be raised by the faithful of the congregation involved. Democracy began here with the collection plate and the right – or better said, duty – to contribute. Those towers and churches were built – or at least paid for – by rich and poor together. The most beautiful gothic church is the St. John's Cathedral in Den Bosch; much of the original beauty has been preserved, in spite of major renovations in the 19th and 20th centuries. It is a testimonial in stone to piety and municipal wealth. Next we leap to the architecture of the 17th century. The Netherlands is literally full of it. One of the most illustrious examples stands in all its glory in The Hague: the Mauritshuis museum, designed by the architect responsible for the Dam Palace and other famous buildings, Jacob van Campen, and begun in 1633 by builder Pieter Post – both men the acknowledged leaders in their fields at the time. Today it is famed as the official home of the royal art collection, as well as many unique and famous paintings not in the royal collection, and is considered a 'must' for all visitors.

We could continue in this manner through the succeeding centuries, but we will leave it here. Those who wish can easily find a similar pathway to their own particular interests that will teach them much about the Netherlands in the process. For, once again, the streets of the Netherlands are the showcases of history.

History, history. It is time to get down to business. There are a couple of useful ways to condense this history into a meaningful context. The development of the Netherlands as a nation, with the battle against the watery elements as a unifying thread running through it all, is one starting point. This line will be pursued in chapter four. It is also possible to hang the pages of history on a line that follows the progress of the country's participation in the community of nations and the democratic freedoms enjoyed by its people. How has the evolution of the Dutch citizen into such a free, open and conciliatory individual come about? This is the thread that will be taken up in the following pages.

There is nothing here about prehistoric times. The Netherlands as a land of people only emerges clearly in the first written records. These were made by the Romans; they arrived in the Low Countries around 57 B.C. They had little interest in the swampy regions of the land. And that is understandable: large areas from the southern Scheldt river to the northeastern Eems formed part of

Aerial photo of an agricultural field near Enkhuizen, North Holland province, on which the surface traces of a farm from the Bronze Age are still clearly visible.

Carefully preserving what the past has left for us. ▼

a remarkable waterscape that consisted of a sort of island chain. This was thinly populated by groups of people living together in small farming and fishing communities on the tiny parcels of dry ground; for them the water was as important as the land since both formed the source of their livelihood. Roads hardly existed; the transport of people, livestock and goods was mainly by water. It would have been extremely difficult to establish a permanent and cohesive rule in this land of the Frisians. The Romans didn't even try. They felt much more at home on the sandy soil of the present day provinces of Limburg, North Brabant, Gelderland and Overijssel. While it is true that they did make frequent expeditions further north, the Rhine was in fact the frontier of the Roman empire. Other navigable rivers, such as the Meuse and the Scheldt, also served as transport routes. Many settlements were established along these. The most important were Maastricht

(Mosa Trajectum) and Nijmegen (Ulpia Noviomagus). The mouths of the rivers were also important. On the island of Walcheren, in the vicinity of the Scheldt's outfall, dozens of sacrificial alters honoring the goddess Nehallennia were discovered in the early 1970s. The Romans were energetic and active organizers and even succeeded in bringing a degree of unity to the territory. They built dikes along the rivers, which were able to serve as fundaments for their highways, and they also dug many canals. In the more than 400 years of their domination they brought the local populations of what is now the Netherlands to a new level of development. They taught new forms of building, of working the land, of shipbuilding and navigation. They maintained a busy commerce between England and western Europe, and even then the Netherlands must have had the function of economic intermediary.

How far did the northern expeditions of the Romans penetrate? A more or less regular trade must have existed with watery Friesland. There may have been a few permanent advance posts: a Frisian place name such as Exmorra – outside the morass – indicates this. Some investigators believe that a Roman game remained behind in the form of the Frisian kaatsen, a tennis-like form of handball that was and is played with hard leather balls filled with horsehair.

Less obvious Roman influences have also been preserved, even if only in the law. In general it can be said that Roman civilization laid the basis for the development of the Netherlands from an isolated, pagan land in which many were unfree and even enslaved, to a free nation that sees itself as a world center.

Did much change in the Low Countries when the Roman power collapsed and they departed from the Rhine delta in about 476 A.D.? The farmer continued to farm, fish and sell what he could. All those fishing farmers and more or less itinerant traders were apparently considered worth going to some trouble for, since christian missionaries did attempt to bring the new faith to them. These had already been active even under the Romans and had already succeeded in converting a small part of the Netherlands, namely south Limburg. In 384 the missionary Saint Servatius was buried there, in the land of the Franks. A church in Maastricht is named after him. Why did Christianity lack the power in those early times to push through to the north? Because the inhabitants of that watery land there wished to remain what they were, free farmers, free fishers. And because they saw the church as at one with outside secular power. Not only did the Frisians in the northwest want nothing to do with the new Frankish faith, also the Saxons in the east reacted hostilely. They feared that the mis-

In honor of the missionary-bishop St. Servaas who lived in the 4th century in Maastricht, construction was begun on a St. Servaas church in that town around the year 1000. This medieval cross basilica was worked on until into the 15th century. For that reason there are several different styles in and on the basilica to be admired today.

23

sionaries would end up revealing themselves as Franks in monks' clothing. And that the Frankish armies would spring up behind the Christian host. In short, personal freedom was at stake. The Frisians and Saxons were proven right. After Charlemagne was crowned emperor by the Roman pope in the year 800, he proceeded to forcefully convert them and subject them to his rule. Whoever tried to resist was exiled or killed. Church and state reigned together.

A new age dawned in the history of western civilization; in the Low Countries a new kind of unity came about, through the christian faith, through the universal though now exclusive Latin tongue shared only by the priests and monks, who established their churches and monasteries everywhere as religious cultural 'monuments', and through the uniformity of the religious rituals wherever they took place. The catholic peace lasted for about seven hundred years. During this period that peace was frequently disturbed, by the many Norman raids as well as by the constant shifts of political power and other factors. But religious unity was maintained, and occasionally even strengthened. Such as during the crusades (11th-13th century) when militarized 'people's' campaigns – organized by church and aristocracy – fought against the rising Islamitic power in the Near East. Hundreds of thousands of farmers, and sometimes even children, marched under the leadership of the nobility to the Holy Land to defend Christianity, and at the same time to reinforce the hegemony of western culture and commercial power, although these concepts and terms were certainly not used at the time.

The consequences of the crusades were far-reaching. Many serfs and bonded servants – we would call them slaves today – won their freedom through participation in the holy wars. As such, this was an important phase in the long, long democratization process. At the same time, hundreds of thousands of 'ignorant' small farmers became aware of completely other worlds, other ways of thinking and other forms of social organization. Not only were the seeds planted here for the later voyages of discovery, for the Renaissance, but also for the Reformation. For the catholic church the crusades had – seen over the long term – a counterproductive effect: people began to think more freely. And it became difficult to impose limits on that free thinking after an important invention in the middle of the fifteenth century: the printing of texts with movable type, which led to the establishment of book publishing. Until that time the duplication of written works had been largely the domain of the monastery brethren, who copied them by hand. Monasteries were therefore also 'publishing' houses. With the new invention the written word emerged from the religious sphere

A praying nun, images of crosses and small chapels along the way. Signs of a still active Roman Catholic faith in the southern part of the Netherlands.

as well and found a place in the secular world of skilled crafts-men, who assumed a respected position in the social order. They began to print texts, at first still religious ones, in the ordinary vernacular, and the interest in being able to read and write began to grow among large groups of the population. The revolution in communications technology was underway. This had major consequences for the development of western Europe. Large groups came of age intellectually. Others – such as seafarers and merchants – had already done so through their broad view on the world. They had long lived with the knowledge that there are many truths in the world. Columbus' discovery of the New World in 1492 flung many other new doors open. Everything changed completely in the second half of the fifteenth century. Many took upon themselves the right to interpret all that was new – and old – in the world in their own, individual manner.

In Germany Luther translated the bible into everyday language. On October 31st, 1517, he initiated, with a few heavy blows of his hammer, a new spiritual climate in Europe. He nailed a protest declaration containing his famous 95 theses to the church door in the German Wittenburg, an act of direct rebellion against Rome. After this, with the support of his ruler and people, his protests against the abuses of power by the church of Rome became steadily stronger. His voice was heard throughout Europe, and ideas of reform gathered momentum everywhere. A new, free age began, filled with vitality, the spirit of discovery and a general appreciation of the arts: the Renaissance.

Why did this blossoming find such immediate enthusiastic expres-sion in the Netherlands? Why did the Reformation have such an immediate success in these Low Countries? Why did a brilliant tradition of painting, a widely acclaimed printing industry, a new approach on all fronts to the natural sciences all flourish so luxu-riantly there?

It is often attempted to explain all of this by the geography of the Netherlands, by the fact that the Low Countries were half water and half land, and that virtually every farmer in the watery pro-vinces of Holland and Friesland was also a fisherman, a boatman, a trader. In that country of lakes and inlets and rivers and a great many islands, a substantial part of the population was not bound to individual villages and towns isolated by the usual lack of roads, but also knew the distant horizons, the tricks of the water-ways, the manners and customs of other towns and villages and – later – other countries. New ideas were nothing strange to them.

The body of water that lies in the heart of the Netherlands, once the Zuiderzee (Southern Sea) and now known as the IJsselmeer (Lake IJssel), was well-known early on in Europe as a large, relatively safe inland sea that was rich in fish. Much more fish could be caught than the local population could consume, and this led to the business of preservation by smoking and salting, and to trade. The fishing boats sailed to distant towns or lands to sell their wares, and returned as cargo vessels, bearing wood or grain from the Scandinavian countries, or salt from Portugal. Thus did the transit trade come into being: fishing villages became commercial port cities and developed themselves as transport and sales centers in a cargo network extending to all points of the compass. The Netherlands, with all those thriving towns on the Southern Sea, and on the rivers, was a traffic junction, a major distribution center. In addition to the many varieties of fish there were also locally produced goods, sheep's wool, cowhides, butter and cheese, earthenware, and a great deal more. The export of herring increased greatly in the fifteenth century after large schools of the fish re-

Old gable stones tell of the fisher and the sea, also of the wife who waits behind.

Fishing nets hanging out to dry on the mast. Tomorrow there will be another catch. ▶

located themselves in the North Sea and even in the Southern Sea. New fishing techniques were then put into use. Much larger nets were created in 1416 in Hoorn, one of the fishing centers on the Southern Sea in an attractive part of North Holland Province known as West Friesland, although it is not within the present province of Friesland. Zeeland in the south also was not standing still. There a herring fisher, Willem Beukelszoon, had developed a degutting technique for preserving salted herring from spoiling for a longer period of time. Wool was increasingly processed and woven into cloth locally. This occured on a large scale in Leyden and on an even larger one in the Belgian – then southern Dutch – town of Bruges. These fabrics were sold far into the Middle East. Amsterdam emerged rapidly in the fifteenth and sixteenth centuries, but had not yet reached its full glory. The center of power in the Low Countries was then still in what is now Flemish Belgium, in the towns of Mechelen and Brussels, where the Burgundians ruled from 1433. In that time the Netherlands still came under the house of Burgundy. The opulent Burgundian court in Brussels had a stimulating influence on many Dutch artists. Just a few names here: the sculptor Claus Sluter, the painters Geertgen tot St. Jans, Dirk Bouts, Gerard David and Hieronymus Bosch. They would become the teachers of the generation of the sixteenth century, of whom Lucas van Leyden and Jan Scorel would in turn become the most famous. In 1515 the Low Countries came under the rule of the Holy Roman Emperor Charles v, who had inherited a vast empire extending from Austria to parts of Spain, which included the just-conquered possessions in the Americas. The Netherlands thus found itself part of a world empire upon which, as has been said of another, the sun never set. The commercial opportunities of the seafaring Dutch were accordingly greatly increased, and it was in this time that the Dutch acquired the name of 'the shippers of Europe'. By the end of the century 2700 sea-going vessels were under sail. They came from many towns, mostly of the Southern Sea, and they were the property of private middle class owners: one ship was usually financed by twenty shareholders, although other arrangements were possible. Not only were the towns locked in competition with each other, but also the individual shipping companies. There was no question of a common commercial policy. This only came about under the pressure of circumstances after the Dutch rebellion against the Spanish rule of the strictly catholic Philip ii, son of Charles v. That was in 1568. Reformed protestant 'heretics' were already being regularly put to death by the religious judges of the Inquisition under Charles v. Under the more Spanish oriented Philip ii the persecution of Dutch protestants became much more merciless. In 1566, to the considerable consternation of catholics and moderate protestants alike, a so-called 'iconoclasm' broke loose. Mobs forced their way into the churches and removed all of the ornate catholic images and religious articles so frowned upon by the dour Calvinists to make the churches suitable for protestant worship. As a countermeasure Philip sent a Spanish army of occupation to the Netherlands. It was under the leadership of a brutal man, the Spanish Duke of Alva, who was made governor and assigned to root out the heresy and to institute a fixed 10% tax to help pay for the army. Thousands fled from the Low Countries, including William of Orange, who had been Spain's leading official for the regions of Holland, Zeeland and Utrecht. Two years later, in 1568, he returned from Germany, this time with a mercenary army of his own.

This first effort against the Spanish ended in complete failure, but would come to be regarded as the official start of the Dutch armed rebellion. The Dutch national anthem, the Wilhelmus (of Orange), harkens back to the battle. Four years later the odds started to change. The first Dutch town fell to the rebels. It was the harbor town of Brielle, captured by privateering Dutch exiles. Today they might be called guerillas.

The war against Spain would last for eighty years. This is not to say that the opponents spent 80 years in the trenches. For one thing, the Spaniards did not have sufficient troops to hold the entire country even if they could have succeeded in subduing it in the first place. For the towns, which were what was being fought over, lay far apart like walled islands in the soggy landscape, which could easily be inundated. By no means did all of the fortified towns side with the rebels. This had not only to do with matters of principle, but also with matters of survival. This explains why Amsterdam, already virtually the strongest city at the time of the uprising in 1568, initially remained on the side of Spain. Such a religious conflict was regarded by the prudent, capitalistic city fathers as highly inconvenient. In addition the Amsterdammers saw the struggle as an opportunity to undercut upcoming competitor towns such as Hoorn and Enkhuizen, which had chosen for the revolt. The Amsterdammers believed that getting involved in a rebellion would do nothing to improve their profit margins. Strangely enough, exactly the opposite proved to be true.

Because the eighty years' war took place for a large part at sea, and there was an ongoing struggle against the Spanish merchant vessels and battle fleet, the Dutch were forced to bring ever better ships into the fight. Through this continuing battle readiness, the Netherlands was by the beginning of the seventeenth century

How the Dutch once defended their cities can still be seen in the form of the town of Willemstad, on the Hollands Diep in North Brabant. The moat around the heptagonal fortification has been excellently preserved.

honed into the most important sea-going nation in the world. The small country overshadowed not just Spain and expansionist Portugal, but all other lands, including powerful England.

The entire Dutch population became, as it were, captivated by a great longing for adventure, a compulsion for conquest, for distant riches. Particularly after Amsterdam went over to the side of the revolt, and many people in the south fled from the Spanish to the independent north, and prominent citizens of Antwerp wanted to invest their money in voyages of discovery, a colonial policy began to be carried out in earnest.

By this time no less than eight different 'overseas' companies had already been set up in different towns. Their aim was the commercial exploitation of the East Indies. They soon began getting in each other's way, which prompted the authorities to merge the existing companies into the United East India Company (VOC),

On the order of the Duke of Alva the counts Egmond and Hoorne were beheaded in June, 1568 on the marketplace in Brussels. Anonymous drawing.

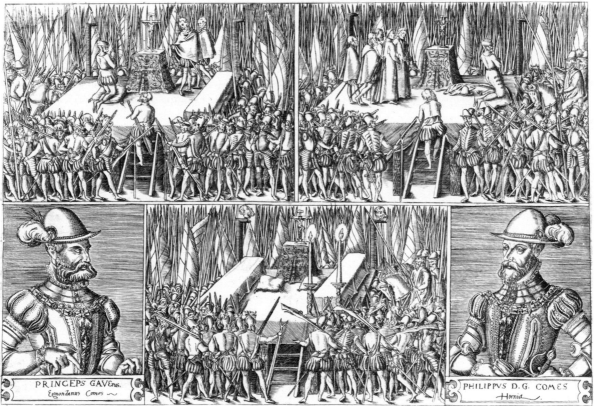

which was granted an exclusive trade monopoly in many parts of the world. Permanent posts were quickly established on the Moluccas, on Ceylon, on Java. The Portugese and the Spanish were squeezed out.

The VOC was a great success, and formed in those days a state within a state. Twenty years later, in 1621, a West India Company was also set up. This company also acquired large possessions, in America on the Hudson (where later New York was founded), along the Gold Coast of Africa, and in Brazil.

The West India Company was to a large extent a pirate operation directed against the Spanish and Portugese. Entire fleets were hijacked by the West India Company. Unimaginable riches poured into the Dutch ports – sometimes even cargos of pure gold and silver, if a Spanish ship had been taken in Mexican waters. It was, with justification, a 'Golden Age'. For millions of people from Africa, however, it was far from golden: the Dutch had an extremely well-organized slave trade from Africa via Curacao to the south of America. With this trade in 'living ebony' huge profits were made. It is worthwhile to occasionally lend a thought to this while admiring the wealth of art from this period in the museums. How did the affluent merchants who paid for these paintings acquire their money? Did Rembrandt van Rijn, Frans Hals, Johannes Vermeer and Jan Steen ever pause over such a question? Probably they were overcome by the exotic luxury of their time, which made the Netherlands the center of the world. Science also flourished with the arts. Christiaan Huygens discovered, along with much else, the pendulum clock and thus the first mechanical means of measuring time with great accuracy. This made it possible, with the subsequent development of less vulnerable timepieces, to precisely determine the position of a ship at sea.

By its very nature, the sea played an important role. 'The Free Sea' – Mare Liberum – is one of the works of Hugo de Groot, who laid the basis of international law, including the principle of the freedom of the seas, in a number of important books. The Dutch certainly had need of this in view of their interference with the populations of Brazil, Angola, Suriname and the Antilles, Taiwan, Sri Lanka, Tasmania, North America, later also Japan from their enclave on the island of Decima; and not to be forgotten, the many people of the Indonesian archipelago. There was hardly any place where the Dutch could not be found after their great expansion around 1600.

The intensive shipping led to a great demand for maps and for accounts of the strange lands. A famous printer was – and still is for collectors – the map-maker Blaue. Other printers also did good business. Many books and pamphlets that writers were not al-

lowed to have printed in other countries were freely published in the liberal Netherlands. The democratization of the free press had already achieved substantial format. The Portugese Jew Spinoza and the Frenchman Descartes enjoyed the hospitality and protection of the republic, where they could develop and publish their radical ideas.

The greatest blossoming of the republic of the seven provinces lasted until into the eighteenth century. In 1668 the then-leader of the republic, William III of Orange, also became the king of England. With this the Netherlands reached its high point of the century. Fourteen years later, however, when William III died, the good times subsided. Gradually the old rival, England, took over the hegemony of the world.

It should not be thought that the prosperity suddenly collapsed after 1702, far from it. The farmer continued to plow his fields, the fisherman continued to haul his rich catches from the sea, the merchant continued to send his ships both east and west. Initially the prosperity even increased somewhat, but less than that of England, which meant a relative decline. A period of consolidation began, of investments in less risky enterprises. For much capital had been accumulated, and that money must be put to work earning dividends. Land reclamation continued here and there, with the laying and raising of new dikes, harbors were improved, cities expanded, roads were laid, and an extensive, well-integrated network of inland waterways, and of coach roads – by no means always paved – made it possible in any case to travel from the north to the south of the seven provinces within a couple of days. Thus did the transport system in the Netherlands – described in glowing terms in many other countries – help to further the unity of the nation. The Netherlands has much to thank the eighteenth century for.

It should also not be forgotten that much attention continued to be concentrated outside the country: the possessions in the tropics were consolidated and investments were even made in foreign countries. When the American colonists declared their independence from England in 1776, Dutch merchants immediately saw great possibilities in North America. A few Amsterdam merchants concluded a treaty with the rebels and invested large sums in their undertaking. Whoever had money could determine politics, and more, could help to give a new nation form. The canals of the northeastern United States, for example, which were dug at the end of the eighteenth century, were partially financed by the Dutch. Shortly after this, however, the Dutch were no longer in a position to contribute anything. The wealthy upper classes had acquired – not only in the Netherlands, but also in France – so much power that a struggle for freedom among less privileged folk began to find voice in the motto: 'liberty, equality, fraternity'. In France a revolution occurred. Shortly thereafter what later came to be known as the 'French period' began in the Netherlands. At first the French ideas, and then the French themselves – under Napoleon – gained supremacy in the Netherlands. In 1804 Napoleon became the French emperor and two years later he appointed his brother Louis King of the Netherlands. Shortly after, the Netherlands was simply made a province of France.

The Netherlands suffered greatly during the French period. Trade came to a virtual halt due to a French blockade put up against their archenemy England. The once-powerful Dutch port towns were still, and what ships there were lay rotting. In 1813, when the French domination came to an end, the Netherlands as a trading nation was in a hopelessly pitiful state. It took a long time for the Netherlands to recover from the effects of the Napoleonic period, in spite of a certain degree of support from England, which saw to it at the peace conference of 1815 – the Congress of Vienna – that the northern and (Belgian) southern Netherlands were joined under the reign of King William I of Orange. This king had excellent business insight and he genuinely had the interests of the country at heart – along with his own, to be sure – but he was more of an 'enlightened' despot than a democratic monarch. And he was certainly a failure as a tactician: in 1830 the Belgians rose against the union. The conflict simmered for nine hopeless and unnecessary years; in 1839 the northern Dutch had to let their southern neighbours go. A year later William abdicated.

Under his son, William II, who was much more popular, a new constitution was introduced in 1848, a time of revolutionary agitation throughout Europe. But that constitution still did not create a democracy such as exists in the Netherlands today. Only well-off citizens (those who paid a certain minimum in taxes) had the right to vote.

For the most part, the 19th century was a difficult time for those men, women and children who possessed nothing more than their labor. Strong drink was cheap and served as a – deceptive – medicine against hunger and cold. Tuberculosis was a common working class disease, limited typhoid epidemics frequently broke out – there was hardly any public water supply. Child mortality was high, and most workers died young.

Against this misery was a gradually growing energy in the country, a spirit of renewal, and an increasingly justified hope for the future. After attempts to stimulate the economy with all kinds of palliatives, such as the digging of new, but much too long canals to the sea, the steam machine finally began to make its presence

Prince William of Orange-Nassau (1533-1584), nicknamed William the Silent and known to the Dutch as 'Father of the Fatherland'. The older portrait was painted around 1583 by an artist whose identity remains unknown.

felt in the economy after 1860 in water control, sugar and potato meal factories, and in the use of steam implements and steam dredgers to dig new harbors and canals for Amsterdam and Rotterdam directly through the dunes, the shortest route. And by about 1880 the Netherlands was genuinely a going concern, with a flourishing textile industry, a food industry that was also strongly oriented towards export, with new factories everywhere, with a growing train and streetcar network, and with continuously expanding cities, where new residential areas sprang up for the office and manual workers. The struggle for full civil rights for the workers, including not only the right to a decent standard of living but also such things as the right to live according to one's own beliefs, took place on many fronts. There was, for example, a long struggle for freedom of education in regard to the right of parents to establish schools that reflected their own convictions. This issue was fought in the first place for the 'little' man, for those of simple outlook and means. The workers received determined support from very different sides, anarchist or social democrat.

In 1919 the eight-hour workday became law and in 1920 the schools issue was resolved with a law putting public and private (religious) schools on an equal financial footing. By the turn of the century the Netherlands – thanks partially to the trade with the East India colonies – had again become a thriving land, with Amsterdam in particular standing out for its cosmopolitan character. The period up to the first world war (1914-1918) was a favorable one for the Netherlands. The dockyards had plenty of work, there was a busy sea traffic to all parts of the world, and even the arts began to blossom again. When the competing industrial countries ended up at war with each other, the neutral Netherlands managed to stay out of it. The Low Countries would only become caught up in the international maelstrom after 1929, when the great international crisis began. The Netherlands, then, in the long, strange, but fascinating century after Napoleon, had certainly become a unified nation for the outside world. But the international divisions – between the working and monied classes, for example – were still great. In spite of compulsory education, working environment safety laws, the eight-hour workday and universal suffrage, there was still much repression and servility. But there was work and bread for everyone. And there was that old, safe neutrality. That would be put to a severe test in the crisis years that followed.

The days of crisis, war and a new prosperity

Many factors were responsible for the collapse of the world economy at the end of 1929 and in the beginning of 1930.

The main hall in the Amsterdam Exchange building, a commodities exchange built around the turn of the century by the architect Hendrik Petrus Berlage, who achieved great recognition with his distinctive style of design.

The number of Dutch who actually lived through the Great Depression is steadily diminishing. Those born in 1929 – the beginning of the 'malaise', as the crisis is often referred to in the Netherlands – are now well over fifty. No one younger than a half-century can have much personal experience of what it was like. It is not a popular period for discussion. To more recent generations it is a reminder of the almost instinctive tight-fistedness of their grandparents and parents, who in their youth were accustomed to counting every penny twice before parting with it. Modern youths have grown up in easier times with plenty of pocket money and the many attractions of the consumer society. Still, the Depression is an important period in recent history. It was in the 1930s that peacetime governments began to involve themselves with the economy on a large scale. The role of government as a major employer – and thus as a major influence on the economy – was broadened. This was also more or less the case in the Netherlands. But in the Netherlands this did not become so clearly evident as in the US, for example, with its New Deal program that was meant to combat the economic depression through the construction of large-scale public works projects. There were many factors responsible for the collapse of the world economy at the end of 1929 and in the beginning of 1930. There was such a complicated coincidence of circumstances that even now it is impossible to say precisely what was going on. In 1929 the Netherlands was not the highly industrialized land that it presently is. There were certainly many long-established industries, as well as much newer ones, such as the steel industry. But the overall pattern was one of development, of emerging growth. The Netherlands had a different economy than its principle neighbors

35

Germany, England and France. The Dutch crisis, then, was not brought about in the first place by domestic shortcomings, but by the economic collapse of neighboring countries. The Netherlands served the function – as it still does – of a distribution and trade center for those countries. For many successive years countless ships passed through the important ports of Rotterdam and Amsterdam. The links with the Netherlands East Indies alone were sufficient to provide important support to the different branches of industry, the stock exchange and the national treasury. Even during the Depression the Netherlands continued to be regarded by its eastern neighbors in particular – the Germans had no colonies to speak of – as 'stinking rich'. The many Dutch unemployed did not exactly share this view. During much of the 1930s, government coalitions were dominated by Hendrik Colijn, the strict leader of the Anti-Revolutionary Party. This fundamentalist Protestant party, set up to combat the secularizing influence of French revolutionary ideas, was one of the several 'confessional' parties that merged into the Christian Democratic party in the 1970s. Colijn, as director of the Batavian Petroleum Company – part of what would later become Royal Dutch Shell – had a classic capitalist mentality and he put his faith in sharp government spending cuts and free enterprise as the means of returning the economy to health. His principle opponents were the socialists of the Social Democratic Labor Party (SDAP), who followed the ideas of the English economist John Maynard Keynes. Accordingly the Dutch socialists had what they called a Work Plan. Keynes felt that massive state funds should be pumped into public works projects to get the machine going again. Colijn opposed the encouragement of a large public debt and the possible stimulation of inflation. He regarded the maintenance of the value of the Dutch currency, the guilder, as the absolute top priority and was determined to keep it 'hard'. To this end he held stubbornly to the 'gold standard' – linking the value of the currency to a fixed amount of gold – even though many neighboring countries had already abandoned this. The result was to make the guilder relatively expensive in terms of competitor currencies, which also made Dutch exports too expensive. Unemployment thus remained high, and wages fell. The burden on the workers was further increased by higher excise taxes, which diminished purchasing power. And this in turn was again greatly detrimental to consumption, thus also production and ultimately, employment. After France, Belgium and even Switzerland had given up the struggle to maintain the gold standard, the Netherlands finally followed in 1936. Gradually, though by no means quickly, things began to go better again. It was a singular time full of contradic-

A new generation.

tions. One paradox, for example, was that many public works projects were in fact carried out under the Anti-Revolutionary governments. The most spectacular of these had already been started long before the crisis, namely in 1920; this was the closing off and draining of the Southern Sea. Although this will be gone into more deeply in another chapter, it briefly involved the following. For about a century different plans had been seriously proposed for this work. One of these came from engineer Cornelis Lely, who had been a minister a couple of times but had never succeeded in getting his plan approved by Parliament. During the first world war he acquired two allies: a flood disaster and a food shortage. Suddenly everyone wanted a safe dike and new lush polder land. In 1918 legislation was passed and two years later the actual work was begun. By the time the crisis broke, the project was well along. In 1932 – in the middle of a time filled with anxiety and unemployment – the 19 mile-long Afsluitdijk (enclosing dam) was completed. It cut off the North Sea from the Southern Sea, which from that date on would be known as Lake IJssel. The first reclaimed polder land, the Wieringermeer, was also readied. The most modern agricultural methods were applied here, and with such success that it was decided in 1936 to reclaim a second polder, the Noordoostpolder. Did Keynes manage to slip into the thoughts of the government after all? Or was this simply a matter of the 'spirit of the times'? Channels were created linking the Maas and the Rhine. New canals were dug in the industrial regions. A link was also established between the Rhine and the textile center in Twente. In addition rivers were made navigable wherever possible. And land reclamation went ahead at an increased tempo along the northern coasts of Friesland and Groningen provinces. A start was made on a tunnel under the Maas in Rotterdam, new bridges appeared over the rivers and canals. A highway network was developed, including a four-lane highway between Amsterdam, The Hague and Utrecht. At the same time, the Utrecht-Arnhem trajectory was laid out. Much was also done on urban renewal and new extensions, and on the laying and maintenance of parks. All in all the Netherlands certainly did not regress in terms of appearance. Much work was also partially or completely carried out through a government employment program, which was in fact a means of getting back some return for the meager compensation paid to the unemployed. But for thousands of other welfare recipients there was no work to be found anywhere. Their only 'employment' was to go stand in the line before the welfare office every day for the control stamp that ensured that they were not also secretly working while on welfare. If wives or children were caught trying to supplement the meager

Socialists (members of the SDAP) demonstrate against increasing unemployment, in The Hague, 1932. On the banner: Capitalism brought us this misery.

This monument marks where the Afsluitdijk (enclosing dam) was closed off on May 28th, 1932 to the loud blasting of all the ships' whistles and sirens present.

37

income by working on the side as household help, the entire family lost its right to aid. There was thus much resentment and much desperation, which even led to civil disturbances in Amsterdam in 1934. The dissatisfaction partially explains why the nazi ideas of Hitler, who had come to power in neighboring Germany in 1933, also found a wide response in the Netherlands. In 1935 the fascist NSB, the National Socialist Movement, received no less than 8% of the vote in the provincial elections. Two years later, during the parliamentary elections, the fascist party fortunately did not secure more than 4%. The great majority had seen the danger and continued to choose for the proven democratic system. There were still strong nationalistic sentiments in the Netherlands, just as in Germany, but these were predominantly economic in nature, the result of the tariff barriers that had been erected throughout the world, to the detriment of Dutch exports. 'Buy Dutch' was a much-heard slogan. In spite of the malaise, Dutch industry in fact picked up after 1936. The light bulb factory of Philips grew into a huge company manufacturing radio sets and other products and became a cornerstone of the national economy. To get around the tariff barriers Philips established foreign subsidiaries in many places. The still-young Hoogovens steel producer near the coast northwest of Amsterdam also grew, and began all manner of ancillary activities such as the production of artificial fertilizers and materials for the construction industry, among other things. In Arnhem and Ede the rayon factories of Enka were expanded. The Dutch/English multinational food products giant Unilever also steadily increased its activities on the domestic market and abroad. And also Royal Dutch Shell began to assume the proportions of a world empire. Seen in this light the slogan 'buy Dutch' did not have much meaning. In the meantime, there was also another slogan, that could be found on socialist doors: 'This door is closed to German goods.' That was purely political.

In the east the aggression of nazi Germany was becoming increasingly more threatening. This aggression had been fueled by the callous way in which the allied powers, particularly France, had treated Germany after the first world war during the treaty of Versailles. Hitler was prepared to take risks and he demanded evermore 'Lebensraum' – the nazi catch-phrase for the aggrandizement of (slavic) territories which they felt Germany had a 'natural' right to. With this he was heading straight for war. In 1936 the Germans occupied the Rhineland in violation of all agreements. In 1936 they also added an entire country, Austria, to the German reich. The next victim was Czechoslovakia, which went under in two phases, in 1938 and 1939. Finally the Germans in-

Without stoplights, with raised intersections to four levels, the important traffic interchange of Leidschendam ensures a smooth flow of traffic to and from the Hague agglomeration.

vaded Poland in 1939. By then England and France had finally had enough, and declared war on Hitler. It would be another eight months before the Netherlands also fell cvictim. That occcurred on May 10th, 1940. The neutral and pacifistic Dutch were hardly prepared. Most had believed, or at least hoped, that Hitler would not bother with the Netherlands, as happened in the first world war. The Germans attacked the sleeping land with a strong force late in the night. It quickly became apparent that the less well-equipped Dutch army was no match for the enemy.

A wave of confusion swept through the Netherlands when, just a couple of days after the war broke out, the queen and the government fled the country together. When the Germans increased the pressure by bombing Rotterdam, capitulation quickly followed on May 15th, 1940. The flight of the queen to the safety of London was at first regarded by many as a betrayal. But this soon came to

The heart of the steel industry Hoogovens at IJmuiden. The molten steel flows from the huge steel cauldron to the dividing trough and from there to the casting moulds. ▶

The considerable international reputation that the Philips concern has accumulated since its founding in 1894 is due in large part to the continuous stream of innovations. Sound and image registration have become a strong point since the second world war. A breakthrough of the so-called 'compact disc' is now being awaited.

be seen as a wise decision instead. Better a Dutch government in exile than one in captivity. Initially, in the first months after the invasion, the behavior of the Germans gave cause to feel that they could easily be lived with, for the civilian government imposed by Hitler was trying to win the support of the population with an accomodating attitude. After the Germans had conquered the French capital and all but crushed the rest of France they had become the effective rulers of the European continent. The chance of a complete liberation – at least in the short term – seemed very slight. In the occupied Netherlands, even though food and clothing were rationed, life more or less went on as before; there were days when one could almost forget that there was a war. There was an air of unreality, even optimism. But those with more insight into world affairs realized that the power of the Germans could continue for years. The first great turning point came in 1941 when America became involved in the war. With some justification the enemies of Hitler again began to entertain hope. At the same time, however, the Germans adopted a hardened attitude towards the occupied territories. For the first time the Dutch were also forced to work in Germany. Professional military officers were again taken prisoner and shipped away. Only the fascist NSB was permitted to remain active as a political party. Members were appointed to important posts. In February, 1941, the residents of Amsterdam rose in mass protest; the strike may have achieved little, but it did show the strength of the Dutch people. Acts of resistance were discouraged from then on not just by imprisonment, but also with executions. It would continue to get worse. In July, 1942, the first Jews were transported to Poland. Initially few dared to guess what was happening there. But slowly a fearful understanding dawned upon increasingly more Dutch people. And with that the underground resistance increased. The most ordinary people, who had never had heroic inclinations, increasingly felt a moral obligation to secretly provide help – with transportation, with money, with food, shelter – to those in danger. The situation that Anne Frank found herself in with her family was not exceptional. Throughout the entire Netherlands Jewish families – and also non-Jews – were hidden in primitive spaces, relying for help on others who in turn were also often dependent upon unknown benefactors, for example to obtain stolen or forged ration cards. It was a highly vulnerable network of brave, but mainly inexperienced citizens, who were not always able to recognize a possible traitor. Life for those in hiding was thus full of constant danger. In addition there was also the awful truth that the war was a very long way from being over. And that it was becoming increasingly difficult to steal ration cards from

Dutch Jews being transported to the collecting camp of Westerbork, in Drenthe, during the German occupation.

40

official offices on a large scale. The prospect of having to look forward to years of existence in cramped and hidden shelters required the utmost discipline from thousands of those in hiding. And no less from those helping them. It is no wonder that many Dutch regarded this exceptional time retrospectively as the most important of their lives. Even those who later emigrated would remain bound to their fatherland by the experiences of danger and comradeship during the war. Not until the end of 1942 was there reason to hope that the Germans would ultimately have to give up

Handwriting from the diary of Anne Frank, the Jewish girl who hid with her family in Amsterdam from June 12th, 1942 until August 1st, 1944 when the family was betrayed. The house where they stayed is now the Anne Frank Museum. Anne died, at the age of fifteen, in March, 1945 at the concentration camp of Bergen-Belsen.

the fight. In November of that year the Americans landed in North Africa. At about the same time the Russians launched a major counteroffensive near Stalingrad. At last the odds in the war turned. But in enslaved Europe life became that much harder. The Germans took over the unoccupied part of France, which made it more difficult to keep the escape routes out of Europe open. For the civil population, including those who would have preferred to keep out of things, the war became total. In the Netherlands all men under the age of 35 had to report for work in Germany. Between June 1942 and March 1943 the Germans transported 163,000 Dutch workers over their border, although this was less than they had hoped since many Dutchmen went into hiding, particularly in the countryside. In all provinces the farmers provided aid and shelter, which meant that the resistance had in fact become wholesale. All kinds of ways were sought to obtain extra

food. There was an extensive black market. Illegal news media flourished. The immediate struggle to survive was supported by the hope for a free future. The miracle of a massive allied landing on the European coasts was awaited.

And that came on June 6th, 1944, a date that millions of Europeans will never again forget. While vast numbers of Americans, English and Canadians perished at Normandy, those in the occupied territories secretly celebrated; freedom was in sight. Just the same, the Netherlands – particularly that part of the Netherlands north of the great rivers – would still have long months of the most wretched misery to go through. While the allies gloriously advanced, the military position of the Germans became more and more critical. They took their recourse in pure violence. In mass razzias Dutch men were plucked from their homes and the streets. Under what were often excruciating conditions they were herded eastwards as forced laborers. In the beginning of September all of France was liberated. After that the allies swept the greatest part of Belgium clean. On September 5th, 1944, it looked as if the big day for the Netherlands had also dawned. On that Tuesday – known to history as 'crazy Tuesday', – the Germans made preparations to withdraw. Great festivities broke out among the Dutch population. The flags were already flying. Too soon! For the advance of the allies was brought to a halt at the great rivers. The Germans quickly picked up where they had left off. Between September and December of that year alone they dragged off another 120,000 men. Such razzias continued to occur until April, 1945. The 'Arbeitseinsatz', as the forced labor was called, was the death of 8500 Dutchmen. In the not yet liberated part of the Netherlands a period had in the meantime begun that would leave its mark on the lives of millions. The Germans brought the supply of food to the still occupied northern Netherlands to a complete halt. What food and material still remained was confiscated for their own war effort. The Germans said this was in reprisal for the general railway strike. This strike, called by the Dutch government in London, had indeed served to hinder the Germans and in this manner to aid the allies. It also demonstrated yet again the value of the government in exile. No one doubted that Queen Wilhelmina was the driving force of that government. A disastrous situation arose in the cut-off, urbanized west of the Netherlands in particular. There were still weekly rations, but these were so meager that they hardly counted. At least as bad was that finally there was no more gas, no more electricity, and water for only short periods per day. There was also no more coal. Small stoves were made from garbage cans in which the scanty meals could be cooked with wood, which was obtained by cutting down all the trees in the cities, stripping abandoned Jewish houses and removing the wooden blocks between streetcar rails. Whoever still had the strength undertook expeditions to the farmlands during this 'hunger winter' to trade valuables or linen goods for food. Sometimes trips lasting days were made, mainly in small groups with primitive transport, or on bicycles with wooden tires. Cats, dogs and even tulip bulbs became prized delicacies. In Amsterdam alone, thousands of people are estimated to have died from famine, while many thousands more succumbed to the exceptionally cold weather. Bodies lay on the streets where they had fallen. Public services had virtually ceased to function and there were no more coffins anyway. Razzias had become part of daily life. The harbors were pointlessly destroyed as a last act of mindless vandalism. It was only in the spring, when the allies continued their offensive, that the still occupied areas were liberated – first the eastern provinces. In the densely populated provinces of North and South Holland, where the food shortage was the most desperate, the Germans had to allow allied aircraft to drop supplies. But before all this food could be distributed to the people, the Germans in the still unliberated part of the Netherlands capitulated. That was on May 5th, 1945. To thunderous cheers the allied tanks rode into Amsterdam, Rotterdam and The Hague. The Dutch people had emerged from five nightmare years. The Dutch sense of solidarity that had been forged by the bloody hammer of the Spanish terror in the sixteenth century, was stronger than ever before. A new, positive nationalism could be felt even on the extreme left. The Dutch came out of the war with a renewed spirit.

The problems directly after the war were enormous. Commerce and industry were crippled, practically all important road and railway bridges in the watery land were destroyed, railway stock and trucks had for the most part disappeared into Germany. The housing crisis created much misery. Little had been built during the depression, let alone in the war. And tens of thousands of homes had been destroyed as a result of the war activities. In addition, more than a quarter of a million Dutch returned from the colonies, mainly the Dutch East Indies, which was seeking its freedom as Indonesia and would cause the Netherlands to become involved in a regrettable conflict over this. Everything taken together, there was little to cheer about. But there was exultation and celebration during the jubilee anniversary of Queen Wilhelmina's 50th year as monarch, when she abdicated in favor of her daughter Juliana in 1948. In fact it was a celebration of national unity. 'Recovery and renewal' were frequently heard words. Everyone wanted to wipe out the traces of the war and work for a

The Hague, March, 1945 after the bombing of the Korte Voorhout.

The festive entry of the Canadian liberators in the days of May in 1945 – here on the Spui in The Hague – left an indelible impression on millions of Dutch people.

new, better country. This was what made it possible to maintain labor peace for so long. Strikes were felt to be inappropriate since this would interfere with progress. Communications between employees and employers in those years, then, were excellent. As early as 1945 the Labor Foundation was set up, a private arbitration body within which, under the watchful eye of the government, negotiations took place between the unions and industry over such matters as working conditions. In 1950 the Social-Economic Council (SER) was established which took over a number of tasks from the Labor Foundation, enabling the latter to confine itself to wage issues. Also of major importance to the realization of the words 'recovery and renewal' was the institution in 1947 of the Marshall Plan, through which American loans were provided for special industrial projects with potential for the future. The stimulating effect of this plan was indeed immense, and provided an effective counterweight to the gloom of the cold war. The fear that the Soviets would sooner or later move into all of western Europe was quite widespread. This brought about a desire to emigrate. It was not only fear that had an influence here, but also disappointment at the difficult progress of reconstruction, and at the same time a desire for more economic freedom and greater private enterprise. Many thousands left the country, mainly for Australia and Canada, but also for America and South Africa. The labor peace, the help of the government and the Marshall Plan, the enthusiasm in the industrial board rooms and the sense that everything was being done for the common good, had such a stimulating effect that by about 1953 the world was beginning to speak in amazement of the Dutch 'miracle'. Even so, the Low Countries were dealt a severe blow in that very year. As the result of a rarely occurring combination of a high spring tide and a northwestern gale on the night of January 31st, the dikes in the southwest of the country were breached in dozens of places. Large parts of the island landscape of Zeeland and South Holland provinces were flooded. Nearly 2,000 people lost their lives, and the material damage went into the tens of millions of dollars. The Dutch people provided aid on a mass scale through a disaster fund, which also received many contributions from abroad. And the Dutch government acted forcefully, first with a rapid and decisive reconstruction – also involving the application of new techniques – and with the drawing up of the all-encompassing Delta Plan, that would provide a high degree of protection to the region, and more. For although the words recovery and renewal were no longer being used, the work was being carried out in the same spirit. The entire plan was fitted into the context of the general notion of 'Ruimtelijke Ordening' (literally, 'arrangement of the

Quick aid from the allies. Food drops in April, 1945 above a liberated area of the country.

physical environment'), a particularly Dutch concept that has materialized in the last years, and which involves a coordinated national approach to matters of the physical environment, such as the optimum use of land, for the greatest good of all. How could space be created for living, work and recreation in the densely populated Netherlands? There were many answers, that together formed a complicated jigsaw puzzle. One of the answers was to proceed at an accelerated pace with the reclamation of land by draining parts of the huge Lake IJssel.

The creating of a 'new' land from the Netherlands was thus being hard worked at, not only internally, but also externally. Already during World War II the Dutch government in exile had sought contact with Belgium and Luxemburg for a closer economic bond, which resulted in the Benelux union in 1948. Along this same policy line lay also the participation in the European Coal and

Insight Holland

Steel Community, Euratom and the European Economic Community (EEC, or Common Market). With this came the transfer in the 1950s of some national prerogatives to international institutions. With that the frontiers of the most important European countries were thrown open to Dutch agrarian and industrial products. Throughout the 1950s things steadily improved for the Netherlands. New agricultural methods increased productivity, more and more factories were built and expanded, the road system grew with the number of cars and vice-versa. Rotterdam evolved into the world's number one port; not last through the increase in the oil trade, the growth of the refineries and the expansion of an increasingly important chemical industry. In many areas it was hardly possible to keep pace with the growth; house building clearly lagged behind demand. To keep the wage structure under control and to prevent inflation the government had a great interest in controlling the housing market and rent levels (relatively few people were home owners). There was a rigid system of permits for obtaining a dwelling. But there was an explosive population growth and demand continued to exceed supply. Whoever had a rental home was as good as rich.

Later, in the 1960s, when huge reserves of natural gas were discovered in the Netherlands and the country, partly as a result of this, became affluent, the banks began to grow more accomodating in granting mortgages for home purchase, and many houses were then built for this purpose, mainly in small communities outside the big cities. This made possession of a car important, particularly for a young, dynamic generation that was no longer prepared to be dependant upon the rigid schedules of train and bus. The lean times of extreme frugality that had dominated the lives of the older folk who had subsisted through the depression and the war years, were over. Now everyone had a right to everything. A new spiritual climate took over in the Netherlands. This climate certainly did not have only a material background. If few people had concerned themselves with foreign affairs before the war, now this was of great interest to everybody. The relaxation of tensions in Russia and the rest of the world after the death of Stalin in 1953 was reflected in the Netherlands by the reduction in the emigration statistics. Practically everyone felt involved in the Hungarian uprising in 1956. In the same year the Suez crisis resulted in a shortage of oil supplies. The Dutch solution – carless Sundays – was accepted with good humor; thousands of strollers, roller-skaters and cyclists took over the highways. Also in 1973, which can be regarded as a real oil crisis, and when the Dutch car population was many times greater, carless Sundays were again accepted without protest. But not because of a lack of spirit. Pro-

February 1953 – a heavy storm and spring tides battered holes in the dikes of the southwestern Netherlands. The sea again flooded the low land.

test demonstrations had in the meantime become a Dutch custom. After the mid-1960s, all manner of individuals and groups attempted to launch both serious and less serious attacks on the consumer society, against capitalist authority and against authority in general. All kinds of anarchistic, often playful movements sprang up against established values and order. Bombs were even thrown during the marriage of Princess Beatrix and Prince Claus. But these were – very symbolically – smoke bombs.

A couple of years later the student movements culminated in direct protest actions which included sit-in takeovers of university buildings. This had already occurred, somewhat more stridently, in France and elsewhere. While the youthful French radical movement reached its climax at the barricades in May, 1968, Dutch offshoots of this phenomenon were more peaceful and thus acquired other forms of expression. In some municipalities playful

On April 30th, 1980, the installation of the 42 year-old Beatrix as Queen of the Netherlands took place according to tradition in the New Church in Amsterdam.

Not everyone was enchanted with the crowning of the new monarch in Amsterdam. Playful protests sometimes escalated into skirmishes with the police. ▶

alternative groups such as the 'kabouters', or 'elves', succeeded in winning a number of council seats in local elections, although they did not retain them for long. The Netherlands soon fell back into its old traditional patterns.

Powerful protest demonstrations, mainly directed against government housing policy, have continued to take place when the opportunity has occurred. The housing shortage is still not completely solved to this day. There are many more small families and single people who want their own homes. And there are many unemployed young people who want decent homes for the little money that they can afford. All that can be said is that the authorities are still trying to find answers to these problems. That the Dutch government does not think only of the welfare of its own citizens, but also that of the Third World countries, is indicated by the contributions that have been made towards development aid. The Netherlands also makes knowledge available, particularly in the area of hydraulic engineering and in that of tropical agriculture. Many foreigners are drawn by the famed International Institute for the Tropics in Amsterdam. In a little over forty years the Netherlands has grown from a neutral, colonial land with a non-militant population to a modern nation that has distanced itself from colonial ties but has, with a much greater degree of self-awareness, taken its place in the center of the world. Someone who had last seen the Netherlands around 1945 would today, at first glance, recognize much that was familiar from that time. But a second look would reveal that the submissive nation from before the second world war had evolved into a population of self-assured, far from mute citizens. The Dutch are quick to put in their 'ten cents' worth' just as, since the Netherlands has become so prosperous, they do in public life with the notion that this prosperity is created by all citizens together.

The bronze statue of an Amsterdam urchin, known as 't Lieverdje ('little darling'), became the focus of regular 'happenings' on the Spui in the 1960s by young people who acquired the nickname 'provos' for the provocative (authority-baiting) nature of their activities.

In the time of 'flower power' the Amsterdam Vondel Park became known in Europe as a meeting place for hippies.

At home in the world

The Dutch have always been formidable travelers, but they are also a homesick nation.

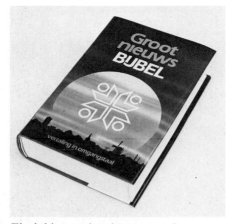

The bible translated into everyday language.

The Dutch are an intimate, homy people. Their homes are not so much their castles as their 'entire world'. When they are at home they are at the heart of things. Why this should be so cannot be explained in a couple of sentences. Probably the bible, and the desire for religious freedom, have something to do with its origins. Was not the home also the church at the time that protestantism first began to gain ground, when it was still illegal? And after the first quarter of the seventeenth century the centerpoint of the protestant home was the reading desk with the Dutch equivalent of the King James bible on it. The world was wherever the bible was. At home, thus. When the bible was opened, there was not only the knowledge of heaven, but also of earth.

Still, the Dutch have always been formidable travelers. With the bible under an arm, they took an important part of home with them. In this manner they never entirely left it. But the goal of all their travel was: to return home again. That is the goal of all fishers: back to home with a full catch. And when some of those Dutch fishers had become traders, it was still the same: back with the merchandise to port, where the warehouse was often also the home. Especially after the Dutch protestants had won religious freedom near the end of the sixteenth century, they certainly had little reason to want to leave their land for good. To travel, certainly. To do business throughout the world, fine. All enterprising folk were in favor of that. But it was most definitely no better anywhere else than in the Low Countries. Peace dominated there. There was space in abundance. Everyone with a piece of ground could more or less get along. And he would not get in another's way: at the beginning of the seventeenth century less than two

51

million persons lived in what is now known as the Netherlands. That explains why the Netherlands exported so few people, and why the Netherlands, yet such a powerful and cultured country, did so little to spread its language. The only place in the world outside the Low Countries – including Belgian Flanders – where anything resembling Dutch, a sort of Dutch, anyway, is spoken, is South Africa. The ships that sailed out from the Southern Sea to the Far East all had to sail around the southern point of Africa. The East India Company began a post there in the eighteenth century, where the ships could obtain fruit and fresh meat, as well as fresh water and vegetables. The people who settled there as farmers did this in the service of the company, and derived their living from the passing ships. And because they had no competition in that beautiful, empty land, some company people decided to settle permanently. The municipality of Amsterdam saw a perfect opportunity to relieve the burden on its overfull orphanages somewhat, and sent a number of orphaned girls, volunteers as it were. The population of the Cape colony began to grow rapidly, especially after that first cargo of orphan girls. Now, after so many centuries, there are in that overwhelmingly black part of the world four million Afrikaans-speaking whites, who also practically all speak English. For after the Englishman Cecil Rhodes found gold and diamonds there at the end of the nineteenth century, the English steadily took over large parts of the Cape, as they had already done off and on before then. Until the beginning of the second world war the Cape remained an English colony. There was also a Dutch colony in North America for a short time. Unlike the Cape, this one was a matter of chance. When the East India Company sent out the Dutch ship 'De Halve Maan' to find a northwest passage to India, the captain navigated an unknown river for this purpose which he gave his own name: the *Hudson*. That was in 1609. When he was unable to continue any further after 125 miles he returned and informed the States-General, then the governing body of the Dutch republic, about the land, which was claimed for the Netherlands. It was given the name New Netherlands. Initially there was not much interest in the new land, except among a few fur traders. The impulse for a more systematic settlement came in 1621, when the West India Company was set up. This company – which was partly a disguised pirate operation and which also conducted a slave trade – received a trade monopoly for the western hemisphere. The first true colonists on the Hudson were however not Dutch, but French-speaking protestants who had had to flee their homeland for religious reasons. For a long time few Dutch had any interest in the colony. Not until the West India Company permitted the colonists in around 1640 to carry on a free trade with the homeland did emigration to the New Netherlands become any more attractive. But it was never a real success. For when the Dutch began to also direct their trade to the English colonies on the American continent, British authority was up in arms: their monopoly was being affected. A British fleet forced the Dutch to surrender in 1664. Ten thousand people then lived along the Hudson and on Manhattan. Only half of these were of Dutch origins. And the common language had already for some time been English. Many adjusted themselves without complaint to the new situation and even Peter Stuyvesant, the former governor, continued to live there. The Dutch continued to use their own language for a long time, especially in their church services. Dutch continued thus to maintain a closed nature, it was in fact a religious language and was never able to replace English. There simply were not enough Dutch there. In fact there were not

Moving with the help of a hydraulic crane is the latest, but hoisting via a block and tackle on the gable has long been a typical Amsterdam manner of getting the furniture in or out.

enough Dutch in the Netherlands itself, at least not enough to crew the great fleets of the East and West India Company. Job-seeking seamen streamed there from all lands, from Scotland, Italy and even Switzerland. They were readily received by the Dutch, who in the ports were already used to all those foreign languages. Not only from their beer trade with the German cities – such as Hamburg – and the grain trade with Scandinavia, but also because of their openess to those with ideas officially disapproved of in their own lands: lutherans, baptists, Mennonites from many different German principalities. The Netherlands thus imported people.

With all those immigrants to the Netherlands came also at the end of the seventeenth century a variety of groups from Baltic ports. Then the Jews arrived, driven out of Portugal by Philip II. The Flemish from the southern Netherlands (Belgium) followed. Afterwards other accents also joined the mix: Yiddish Poles. From France came the Huguenots; many French-sounding names in the Netherlands are reminders of this. The Netherlands itself benefited considerably from the import of all these people and ideas… because all these different viewpoints had a stimulating influence on each other and prevented a possible spiritual inbreeding in the small land. And because this import gave the Dutch the feeling of being at the center of the world in their own *home*, a baroque, universal feeling that is expressed so strongly in the work of Rembrandt and others. They also later discovered the whole world in Amsterdam, did they not? Some went, others stayed. Together they created the atmosphere of their own Amsterdam. And of a number of other Dutch cities: Haarlem, for example, Delft, Leiden, Dordrecht. They invested or they worked as craftsmen, and they enriched the multifarious diversity that has always been a characteristic of the Netherlands. The eighteenth century was also characterized by a fertile interchange; many different kinds of foreigners were continuously present in the Netherlands, while the Dutch were continuously present in many foreign countries. In Japan, for instance, or at least an outpost of it – the artificial island of Decima – the Dutch were permitted, as the only outsiders, to establish a trading post as early as 1636. That special link between Japan and the Netherlands continued throughout the entire eighteenth century. It was only after 1854 that Decima lost its exclusiveness and Japan opened its door wider to outsiders.

The eighteenth century was also important for the strengthening of the Dutch power in the Indonesian archipelago. Then the cultivation of sugar cane began to be stimulated, next to the already old crops of coffee, tea and spices. With that, industrialization also began in that country: small sugar factories sprang up

Of the Dutch who emigrated in 1982 most went to Australia (2,394). 1,970 emigrated to Canada, 1,250 to New Zealand and 381 to America. If we look at the figures over the period from 1946 through 1982, we see a clear shift. The total numbers of emigrants during this period to Australia, Canada, New Zealand and America were respectively 154,323, 184,150, 34,733 and 89,030.

Portrait of Hendrickje Stoffels, painted in 1660 by Rembrandt van Rijn (1606-1669).

View of Delft, about 1658, painting by Johannes Vermeer (1632-1675). ▼

everywhere. In addition the Dutch continued to do business with Taiwan and they occupied a very strong position in Sri Lanka, the former Ceylon, where they controlled the coast until the end of the eighteenth century, while they were also on good terms with the inland kingdom. Many Dutch tombstones and a number of buildings still serve as reminders of that Dutch period, which came to an end as a result of the Napoleonic administration in Europe. The English emerged from the power struggle as the winners, and thus also established themselves on Tasmania (named after the Groningen explorer Abel Tasman), which had long lain in the Dutch sphere of influence. What was it like in the South American territories? Brazil, one of the most important lands on this continent, which had briefly linked its future to that of the Netherlands, namely under Johan Maurits van Nassau, who was governor there from 1636 until 1644, remained tightly in Por-

tugese hands during the eighteenth century. But in the Caribbean area the Dutch retained their influence, also on the continent, in Suriname, where especially in the eighteenth century – the century of consolidation – many plantations were established, not only by the Dutch rulers but also by French Huguenots and Portugese Jews. In 1795 Suriname became part of the Dutch state. Only nearly two centuries later, on November 25th, 1975, did Suriname become independent. Thousands of Surinamese had in the meantime chosen for continued Dutch citizenship and permanent residence in the Netherlands.

Of great importance for the Netherlands were the Antilles, particularly the island of Curacao, which thrived during the eighteenth century, not least because of an intensive slave trade with North America in particular. Curacao played an important part as a supplier of weapons – or at least as a link in the supply chain – in the anti-colonial struggle for independence of the Americans in the seventh decade of the eighteenth century. This period of prosperity would not return after the fall of Napoleon in 1815 and a strong decline even set in after the abolition of slavery. In the twentieth century the island again became important, especially for the oil industry. Curacao is still – in a rather loose way – tied to the Netherlands. Dutch is spoken and written there. The widespread Dutch influence did not result in a mass exodus of the Dutch to all those exotic worlds; there was no emigration of significance. It would take until 1846 before the Netherlands became a large-scale exporter of human potential; of impoverished country folk who, for religious reasons, may not exactly have fled their country, but were certainly happy enough to leave it. How could this have happened? Under the reign of William I, the first Dutch king, the constitution guaranteed religious freedom. At the same time, only the official state church, the Dutch Reformed Church, received state support. Although Roman catholic religious services were not made impossible, they were restricted. This was even more true of a group of protestant dissidents that had split off from the state church in 1834 on extreme fundamentalist, orthodox Calvinist ground. They opposed the rigid authority of the official church and the wealthy controllers of it. They had few means for this, since they mainly came from the poorest sections of the population. Their theological revolt also had clear social elements, and the state saw these as such: military counter-measures, even prison sentences, were not unusual. In 1846 and 1847 two groups of dissidents and one group of Roman catholics left for the United States. Why there? Because their path had already been smoothed by Amsterdam investors and bankers who since 1782 had been involved in the placing of American loans on the Am-

William I (1772-1843), after the Napoleonic occupation the first king of the Netherlands.

56

In the seventeenth century, Dutch sea-farers brought back reports of their journeys to the East Indies.

The twelve-volume *Library of the Indies* (The University of Massachusetts Press) presents in English translation, with critical introductions and notes, a substantial body of the literature that arose from the encounter of the Dutch with the tropical Indies, during a period of over three centuries. It includes narratives of journeys, histories, nature studies, essays, and novels. It is a literature of great creativity and irony, a record of the lost causes and expectations of a colonial power.

A volume in the series is *Max Havelaar* by Multatuli. First published in 1860, Max Havelaar is a powerful indictment of colonialism. Translated into over fifteen languages and the subject of a recent film, the novel ranks with the classic works of E.M. Forster and Joseph Conrad in its depiction of the virulent European subjection of foreign peoples, in this case the Javanese. The story is based on the life of Multatuli (Edward Douwes Dekker, 1820-1887), one of Holland most honored writers, and builds on the conflict between the materialistic coffee broker Drystubble and the idealistic protagonist who is martyred for his struggle against

sterdam money market. In 1795 they set up the *Holland Land Company*, which purchased land in the states of Pennsylvania and New York. The intention was to resell this land at a profit to the stream of colonists whom it was still hoped could be enticed to come. There was also a financial involvement in the digging of the Erie Canal, which gave New York a shipping link with the Great Lakes. The city of Buffalo, at the end of the canal, was itself founded by a small colony of the Holland Land Company. This American expansion to the west, and the resulting acquisition of new, fertile agricultural lands, led to an American grain surplus which the small-scale European farmers could not compete against. In addition people in the old world were having to contend with a disease afflicting the potato, which had become a staple food for the masses. In the first half of the nineteenth century a crisis situation occurred. German farmers and workers first fled their impoverished land to the USA. And then came the groups of Dutch emigrants. With them, religious factors were initially the strongest motivation, but economic considerations also played a role.

The poorest group of dissidents, under pastor Van Raalte, started from scratch in the woods of Michigan. The colony Holland, which would later become quite successful, was established there. A second group, under Pastor Scholte, left the home country under somewhat more prosperous circumstances, and was in a position to buy already prepared agricultural land. This happened in Iowa, where the colony Pella came into existence. The group of catholics, under Father Van den Broek, settled in Wisconsin, in the area of Little Chute. These settlements have had a strong attraction on kindred spirits from the home country. Increasing numbers of Dutch emigrants crossed the Atlantic ocean. New colonies, in many states of the USA, were established from the existing ones. In 1850 ten thousand Dutch had already emigrated. The protestants continued for a very long time to hold their religious services in Dutch, in some places until after the second world war. But gradually the battle against the new, English-speaking generations had to be given up. Later, when cheap agricultural land became scarce in the US, religious groups emigrated to the cheaper Canada as well. Also there the language could not be maintained, though the struggle was kept up for a remarkably long time. In the meantime an entirely different sort of 'emigration' had got underway in the nineteenth century: the dispatching of planters, administrators, soil experts, biologists, doctors, teachers and soldiers to the Netherlands East Indies, later also called Insulinde. There, in that sparkling island chain, the Dutch population grew so strongly that even a Dutch newspaper industry was the injustices of the colonial administration.

The other eleven volumes are:

Faded Portraits by F. Breton de Nijs

The Poison Tree: Selected writings of *Rumphius on the Natural History of the Indies* by E.M. Beekman

Mirror of the Indies: A History of Dutch Colonial Literature by Rob Nieuwenhuis

Country of Origin by E. Du Perron

The Hidden Force by L. Couperus

The Islands by A. Alberts

John Company by A. van Schendel

The Ten Thousand Things by Maria Dermoût

Ups and Downs of Life in the Indies by P.A. Daum

An Anthology of the Literature of the East Indies by E.M. Beekman

The Last House in the World by Beb Vuyk

The Counselor by H.J. Friedericy

able to flourish. Nearly all the Dutch there developed a close bond of affection for Insulinde, for the opportunities, the splendid landscapes, the friendly people, the often fairy tale atmosphere, which provided Dutch literature with exotic impulses for a good century. The Dutch in Insulinde lived in a state of permanent nostalgia: for 'Holland' when they were sitting under the hot sun, and for the Indies when they were on leave in the Dutch rain. After 1945, when the Indies received the name of Indonesia, about 250,000 Dutch or Indonesian Dutch returned to the home country. Filled with homesickness, they left 60 million (now 150 million!) Indonesians behind. A large number of Indonesian Dutch were able to settle later in the United States, and they did this mainly in California, where the climate was more attractive to them. That occurred at the same time as the great overall emigration wave from the Netherlands that took place in the difficult years after the second world war. Virtually all of these emigrants, whether to America, Canada, South Africa, Australia, or wherever they went, attempted to integrate themselves as quickly as possible and they immediately took English as their new language. By this they attempted to put the old country firmly behind them. The Dutch were much more rigorous in this than the Poles, the Irish, the Italians, the Greeks, who continued to maintain strong ties with each other and with the former homeland. The Dutch on the other hand chose once and for all for their new homeland – their new home – and attempted to live with the feeling that 'homesickness is better than Holland', as the poet Leo Vroman has said. That has become a catch-phrase in the Netherlands, but it does not fully dispose of the subject. The bonds between practically all post-war emigrants and their fatherland, particularly their friends and relatives, have remained extremely close. However hard the emigrant tried to be loyal to his new land, the emotional ties with the old were practically impossible to sever. Because of this the availability of cheap, or at least affordable charter flights increased enormously in the 1960s. Many emigrants made the trip to the fatherland for a short vacation, felt themselves none the less somewhat displaced there, and went back with the feeling that they had still made the best choice. But sometimes the opposite feeling took over. In cases of uncertainty the visit of the family often helped. Particularly in the 1970s, when flying became steadily cheaper, and the feeling grew on both sides that only a few hours separated them, the burdens of emigration became much lighter for many. Those entertaining thoughts of emigration now had, unlike before, the possibility to take a look at the land of their choice. For that reason emigration – in so far as it is still possible in this time – has become much less of a gamble. It has been calculated that the

Netherlands – now with more than fourteen million people – would have had at least a million people more had it not been for the government's emigration policy. Every emigrant was in principle eligible for a government grant. This naturally involved considerable sums. The question is: Did the Dutch nation gain anything by this? Probably it did. For all of those Dutch emigrants together have given the word *Dutch* a powerful, positive significance. Whoever is Dutch is a hard worker, is thrifty, and is trustworthy. His word is his word of honor. These attitudes about the Dutch have been built up by the emigrants collectively. For the traveling Dutch businessman that image opens many doors: he is usually welcome in advance. On the other hand, the Netherlands could well have used the many capable emigrants itself. More than a half-million people were imported from the lands around the Mediterranean Sea in the years of great prosperity and labor shortage as 'guest workers' to take over the mainly menial tasks that the affluent Dutch were no longer willing to consider. Even when the prosperity began to ebb away many Turks, Greeks, Spaniards, Italians, Algerians, Moroccans and others decided to stay on. A large number even opted for Dutch citizenship. A notable integration has not, however, been achieved. The authorities have also not pushed too hard for this. Many of these people have been unwilling or unable to abandon their own strong cultural and religious traditions for the sake of assimilation into Dutch society, while many Dutch have been equally unwilling to accept their 'guests' as full and worthy citizens. There has thus been no notable influence of the immigrant workers on the Dutch language, such as the Jewish immigrants had with their Yiddish. What has changed is the interest in foreign cooking. The predominance of the Dutch mashed vegetable pot is a thing of the past. There is an abundance of small, exotic and mostly very reasonable restaurants in the Netherlands: Greek, Turkish, Moroccan, and practically every other kind of food imaginable is readily available, and, as in the past, also Indonesian and Chinese, of course. In the last ten or fifteen years Surinamese cooking has also been added. This thanks to the large influx of Dutch Surinamese who, in the years preceding the independence of their tropical land, ultimately chose for a life in the Low Countries. Again, thus, a homesick generation. Have the Dutch changed? Has the departure of family and friends damaged their nation? Has the coming into being of a new Babylon disturbed their peace? The answer to all these questions is probably no. The Dutch have remained much the same. They still very much enjoy traveling, but they enjoy sitting at home even more.

A heritage of colonial times. In addition to about 25,000 South Moluccans from the former East Indies (Indonesia), more than 150,000 Dutch from Suriname ('West Indies') now live here.

How different is the Dutch day

The Dutch fill their days with almost the same activities as their European neighbors. Only the way in which they do these things is different.

How do the Dutch spend their days? Just like everyone else in the western countries. By getting up, having breakfast, going to school or work, carrying out their tasks to their best ability, returning home, having the evening meal together, spending the rest of the evening studying or taking it easy, letting the dog out afterwards, and finally turning back the blankets and going to bed. But the Dutch do all these things just a little bit differently than their European neighbors. The average Dutch family is small. One child is usually too few, three, more than enough. Everyone is affected to some degree in one way or another by the overpopulation, in traffic, on the beaches, shopping in the city. The Netherlands is indeed a chock-full land, particularly in the large urbanized region of the west known as the Randstad. Land there is expensive and the houses, especially in the residential districts with apartment blocks, are not as big as everyone might like. Foreigners, especially Americans and Canadians, are often surprised at how cramped – by their standards – even well-off people live in the inner cities. Still, these accomodations are equipped with all the modern conveniences. For nearly twenty years all new dwellings have come with central heating, efficient kitchens, and well-equipped bathrooms. Generally one per dwelling, so the use of washing facilities in the morning is a matter of organization, even in small families. The cleanliness of the Dutch forms an interesting subject. For a long time the Dutch nation proclaimed that its people were so clean.

This was also true: on the outside. Windows were constantly washed and the front steps scrubbed. Until 1935, though, newly-built mass housing still contained *no* bathing facilities. Either the

61

washtub was filled on Saturday or a visit was made to the public bath-house which existed in every city. That is no longer necessary. In every new house one can take a shower or bath. Younger people do that every morning if they live alone. Their parents still often find that it costs too much water and energy. The traditional family is on the decline in the Netherlands. According to the most recent national statistics (end 1981) only 43% of all households still fit the old-fashioned image. The old-fashioned household routine has thus also changed accordingly. The more than one million people who live alone are more likely than not to skip the breakfast ritual altogether and make do with a cup of strong coffee before rushing off to work in the morning, assuming they still have a job to go to. An imaginary 'average' family will probably still sit down to breakfast together, a simple affair based on bread. Two kinds of bread, brown and white, are usually eaten. The Dutch still buy their bread fresh from the bakery, where it is usually baked on the premises, and whole meal brown bread varieties have become increasingly popular with the growing awareness of healthy life-styles. Sometimes there is also traditional unleavened rye bread. The choice of what to put on the bread is not great in the morning. At least not at home. In many hotel restaurants a more extensive breakfast can still be had, but the middle class family makes do with jam, peanut butter, cheese. And with one or another of the typically Dutch sprinkled treats: chocolate flakes or the more colorfully named 'hailstorm' (hagelslag) and 'little mice' (muisjes). Like the flakes, hagelslag is made from either natural or milk chocolate. It comes in the form of a fine chocolate string chopped into small lengths. A single slice of bread is always spread with margarine or preferably butter, which has the reputation of being expensive. Even some dairy farmers use margarine for their meals on bread, and its use has become so widespread that it is even commonly referred to simply as butter. The Dutch breakfast is a silent occasion for everyone is usually in a hurry. If the weather is good, and a streetcar stop is not too far away, the car may be left behind. That saves money and frustration, since Dutch traffic in the morning rush hour is no fun. If children have to travel far, they take the bicycle. This is the cheapest mode of transport as well as a traditional one for the past eighty years. This has come about because the country is flat, the distances between residential areas and the factories, offices and schools always coverable, and because the authorities began very early with the laying out of a finely meshing network of cycle paths. In the mornings the Netherlands presents a picture of tens of thousands of children all on their way to school by bicycle. In the countryside they often cover distances of ten miles or more in

each direction. Small children, as well as adults, are also used to this form of transport. In the beginning they are brought to the kindergarten by one of their parents in a special baby seat mounted on the bicycle. Later the children are allowed to cycle themselves, but still under the supervision of an adult, like ducklings following their mother. Finally they are allowed to go on their own, always a risky undertaking in the busy Dutch traffic. There are separate traffic regulations regarding cyclists, but there are also impatient drivers, with all the consequences of that. While everyone is busily underway, the typical Dutch housewife is probably busy with her housekeeping in a very old-fashioned way. Less than half of Dutch women have a job, and many of these work only part-time. That this is not entirely a matter of choice is indicated by the increasing numbers of officially unemployed women who are registering with employment offices as job-seekers, but the percentage of working women remains much higher in neighboring countries. Does this mean that the Dutch woman is simply a drudge chained to her kitchen? Has emancipation had no effect on her?

Women have had the right to vote since 1918. They have also long been active in Parliament and there are female ministers and underministers, although these remain very much in the minority. Various feminist movements have also emerged in recent years and there is a vocal feminist minority active in the country. At the same time, the great increase in prosperity has certainly made the task of the traditional housewife much lighter and this had made it physically easier at least for some women to continue to choose for their traditional role. Others, however, have little choice because of economic factors, a still-dominant traditional mentality that severely restricts their opportunities to change their life-style, and a lack of adequate educational opportunities when they were attending school. Many are also struggling to raise children on their own, which can form a serious obstacle to their employment prospects. More than 12% of all families with children are now single-parent households, and practically all of these single parents are women. Many have what is at best a bleak subsistence existence as a result of massive and continuing government cutbacks in welfare support, which have hit them particularly hard, and they would undoubtedly be glad to have a job if they could succeed in finding one. Emancipation is as much an economic issue as a social one. A Dutchman who emigrated 35 years ago and returned now to see how the Dutch were getting on, would thus find in many cases that the housewife was still in the house, whether by choice or not. A familiar image. But her circumstances would be completely changed. No coal heaters any longer, no ash

Airing the bed linen is an ideal occasion to catch up on what is going on in the street.

Insight Holland

Many working women do administrative work with little career opportunity. With banners such as 'We Women Demand' the women's movement demonstrates for equal opportunities and equal pay.

residue, no coal dust through the entire house. Now there is central heating. The stranger will not know that there was also an oil heater for a time – even that was already a great improvement – and soon after that a gas heater, and now heating in all the rooms. In the middle of the 1960s all of the Netherlands was connected to an immense natural gas reservoir that had been discovered in the north of the country. By that time many Dutch already had a car. They nearly all had a television and a view of the world. In the same period the birth control pill became available to everyone. While not all women used it, all did discuss it. A new kind of freedom came into being. A whole complex of factors combined to make the Dutch more free in a couple of years than they had ever been: the pill, the centrally heated house (also the bedroom), affordable showers through cheaper gas, frank information on all matters through the television, vacation bonuses and the car

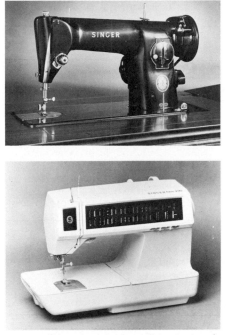

'Singer, slinger, sewing machine,' according to poet Paul van Ostaijen in the first quarter of our century. The device had then already been popular for many years, as the Singer Manufacturing Company (1867) *had succeeded in selling the product throughout the world.*

Recycling of old glass. In many cities and villages there are bins for different kinds of glass to deposit empty bottles and glass jars in.

before the door. Everyone was a respectable burgher. But some old ideas and customs have not yet died out. Such as the notion that the woman's place is in the home, at least as long as there are still children to be raised, although this outmoded attitude has little relevance in the modern situation. The instinctive Dutch thriftiness also remains strong. Every Dutch family still has a sewing machine, the first mass-produced machine, it might be added, to find its way into the Dutch home – even before the bicycle. A little bit of history: natural gas was present early on in the Netherlands, at the end of the last century already. Every city had its gas industry. Running water also existed, although not everywhere in the countryside. That only came in the 1930s. The flush toilet became common for the less affluent as well after the first world war. In that time the first hand-operated washing machines began to catch on. And the vacuum cleaner arrived. What has been added since the second world war? Automatic washing machines, dryers, ever-larger refrigerators, freezers, electric ovens, microwave ovens. What disappeared was the old-fashioned broom, the window sprayer, the unhandy coffee grinder, the ribbed wash-board, the zinc basin, the copper bottle, the screened food cupboard on the balcony. But what remained, permanent and unchanged – though motorized – was the Symbol of Thrift, the sewing machine. A hundred years ago the Netherlands was predominantly a farming community with a few larger and smaller towns here and there. Little of that remains: only 6% of the population is still directly employed in the agrarian sector. The remainder has been fleeing to the cities since 1880 at an accelerating rate, to an industrial world, an entirely different way of life. Little can still be detected of the old farming customs. With some difficulty traces of earlier eating habits can still be found. Breakfast, as we have already seen, is light, in contrast to the classic heavy farmer's breakfast of bacon, pancakes and porridge. Pancakes are now no longer made for breakfast. Here and there a bowl of oatmeal or a lighter cereal may still be eaten. Quite popular is *muesli*, a mixture of whole grains, dried fruit and honey. But widespread this breakfast is not. In short, the farmer's breakfast has disappeared in the cities. Other things are still familiar, in some small, provincial towns. There the main meal of the day – the 'warm meal' – is taken in the afternoon, at around 12:30. The maintenance of this custom is dependent on the distance between work and home. In the urbanized west, however, where more than half of the Dutch population lives, lunch consists of something on bread.

And what about at work? That depends on the income and the job of the employee. It is common for a working man to take a lunch box with sandwiches, an apple and something to drink along. That is still always the cheapest. But in many companies the cantines are very inexpensive. With the lunch a great deal of milk, the national drink, is consumed. This is not only due to the country's farming background but certainly also to the unrelenting advertising campaigns. Famous people recommend the national product in the newspapers and on television. 'I drink milk, you too?' The dairy industry is very active. With that we have not finished with the afternoon meal. Just the opposite. If guests should drop in during the afternoon, friends or relatives, then the hosts go all out. The cold meal in its optimum form can best be seen on a Sunday, if everyone is present, and there are perhaps also visitors, and everyone sits down to a well-spread table, which Americans would call 'brunch'. Here the history of the countryside suddenly presents itself, for practically every province is famed for its own special 'coffee table'.

Many restaurants also serve a coffee table. Such an extensive cold meal is most pleasurable enjoyed in a large company, for example during an excursion, a conference or an official reception. The provincial restaurateur will then arrange for waitresses in the traditional folk costume of the region, and for specialties: 'Limburgse vlaai' – a fruit pastry, or 'Friese eierkoeken' – small rich cakes made with eggs, or 'Drentse bollen' – a kind of raisin bread, 'Groninger gemberkoek' – a kind of ginger cake with pieces of candied ginger in it. In the northern provinces the old-fashioned 'kraantjespot', a round-bellied Frisian tin coffee pot – decorated or not – with a tap near the bottom from which the coffee is poured will also always be present on the table.

Those who still remember the Netherlands from just after the second world war will recall that Monday was always washday. In the countryside in particular there was always an intense competition to see which of the women in a neighborhood would be first to have the week's washing hanging on the line to dry. With so little privacy, every woman felt obligated to display the whitest wash. The Dutch also have a saying about keeping the dirty linen out of sight. Tuesdays or Wednesdays were ironing days, by which time the wash would be dry if the weather had been co-operative. There were also other set days: Friday was for washing the windows, scrubbing the sidewalk and polishing the copper doorknob. In the country this still occurs, but it is no longer an iron duty. And on Saturday it was the turn of the people. Sundays everyone went to church. 'With a bible inlaid in silver', as an old Dutch rhyme says. In the Netherlands church-going also did not have only a religious, but a social function as well. The clothing, the hats, the shoes, the silver-lined handbags, the design of the

The coffee table is characterized by abundance. In addition to many different kinds of bread, (both brown and white, in all varieties and sizes, rye bread, raisin bread and gingerbread), there is a large choice of spreads. Cold meats such as ham, salami, roast beef, seasoned raw hamburger known as 'tartaar', typically Dutch processed meat products such as 'cervelaat' (a sausage made of smoked pork), 'pekelvlees' (boiled salted beef) and 'gelardeerde' liver (with pork in it), liver paté, and many different kinds of fish such as lightly salted herring, smoked eel, or smoked mackerel. Liver and pekelvlees together on bread also form a national specialty, a sandwich known as 'half-om'. Then there are the many Dutch cheeses, aged and unaged, perhaps with cloves or caraway seeds. And quite often there is also a warm snack (for example a croquet) or there is a hussar salad as a cold dish.

psalm and hymn books were just so many signs of this. Many marriages arose from meetings in or around the church. Church attendance has fallen sharply in the last quarter-century, but those who still go do that now less for social reasons than truly religious ones. From the electric iron to religious observance, for everything ties together; with the greater personal freedom made possible by increasing affluence and labor-saving devices came also another vision of church and god. The new prosperity also had its influence on *interior design*. The history of Dutch home furnishing is a history of the desirable versus the possible. On the one hand the small living spaces have not made a spacious, modern design possible, while on the other, only a small elite has striven for this. The home of more well-off Dutch is distinguished from that of the foreigner with a comparable standard of living by a certain unconventional intimacy. But it is in fact a hybrid, a mixture of a bit of modern with a bit of classic.

In the years between the two world wars the Netherlands became a land rich in designer talent. The architectural ideas of *De Stijl*, of painters such as Mondrian, builders such as Oud, Rietveld, Dudok and Duiker have had at least as much influence on the world as the *Bauhaus* in Germany has. In that period large and truly modern residential districts were created in the Netherlands. Public taste, however, was hardly influenced by that avant-garde. No wonder that rattan furniture was so popular after the war: it was a familiar thing, by its nature already a bit exotic, but also not so uncompromisingly modern in its new design as to be shocking. For the Dutch the living environment should not express revolutionary ideas: it's language should be reassuring, pleasant, warm. A 'little' unconventional is acceptable but no more. The home may well be the Dutchman's 'world' – as we have seen – but it is a neutral, bourgeois world. Its message is intimacy. In the 1970s a reactionary trend, the 'hand-me-down' style, did find place, particularly among younger people. This fashion can be partially explained as a reaction to the widespread demolition and renovation of old, inexpensive working-class residential districts, and even entire city centers, as was the case in Utrecht. Until that time the Dutch were used to low rents. Whoever married and finally became eligible for an apartment was happy to accept all the faults that came with it. People fixed their places up themselves as best they could, with a shower stall in the kitchen. At least they had a place to live. And it was a place they could afford. After 1965, when the large gas discoveries in the northern Netherlands made mass central heating possible, and housing acquired a completely different, much more spacious arrangement partially as a result of this, house-building everywhere took on a more enjoyable, cheer-

The housing estate of Spangen (1919-1921) in Rotterdam, built under commission of the municipal housing authority, was designed by M. Brinkman. An existing street was incorporated into the closed-off estate. The houses are reachable via galleries, broad enough for deliverymen with their carts. It has served as an example of public housing for many later architects.

ful form. The old working-class neighborhoods began to appear even older and more primitive, completely outmoded, in fact, and the progressive city fathers stimulated demolition and rebuilding, or at the very least, renovation. The building societies improved kitchens, installed central heating, renovated bathrooms, ultimately this resulted in higher rents. A wave of protest swept through the land. Suddenly there was mass opposition to all that modernity. A widespread softening of attitude towards the old set in. For the manner in which previous generations had lived. Articles from grandfather's time became almost sacred: manufactured carpets fifty years old, dark overcurtains, oval portrait frames, grandma's cupboards, yellowed photographs, and even 'stoven', wooden footrests in which glowing embers could warm the feet. Women began going around in long, flowered dresses from before the first world war, and everything was nostalgia, and swearing by the old, and the affordable. And affordable it was. The new prosperity made it possible for hundreds of thousands to refurnish their homes. Often the well-off put their old, pre-war furniture on the street for the garbage collector. Thousands of young people furnished their homes then with items that they found for free by the garbage. And what did the better-off citizens do in that time? They followed the trend – somewhat – and acquired antiques, but then real antiques, Frisian clocks from 1850, Empire furniture, linen cabinets guaranteed to be a century old. Suddenly everyone was an expert.

Afternoon tea is still a common tradition in the 'typical' Dutch family. As the nation's school children migrate homewards on their bicycles in their hundreds of thousands the teapot is set out on a warming candle and some cookies are put out on a dish. It is an old tradition, tea with a cookie at four o'clock. It resembles the English tea a little, but that has more of the substance of a real meal. Sometimes the children may be given an apple or banana, or a filling sandwich to keep them going until six. The children will usually each have their own room nowadays and they will retire there to do their homework. There is compulsory education until the age of seventeen, and the educational level followed will determine what one is able to do afterwards. Dutch secondary education, though under review, is still narrowly channeled along different vocational and specialized lines, but the former certainty of having a pre-determined slot to fit into at the end of the process no longer exists. The universities, for which only a portion of students are qualified by their secondary education, are overly full and there are often admission quotas that keep more out than they let in. Unskilled or semiskilled work has little appeal since there is already mass unemployment among young people. There is a

The so-called 'rotan furniture' was extremely popular in the Dutch living room in the 1950s. It was practical, affordable, and it had an airyness that went well in the small living rooms of just after the second world war. Typical is the irregular placing of the furniture, by which it was attempted to achieve a sense of 'gezelligheid'.

measure of welfare support for the young unemployed, but this is being increasingly curtailed and it offers little perspective for the future. While there is a shortage of skilled workers in some professions, the educational system has not yet been able to adjust itself to cope with the new situation.

At around six it is customary to drink a 'borrel' or two, usually the distinctive Dutch gin, genever. These days it is not uncommon for a husband and wife to share this pleasure together, although in earlier times, up until about a quarter of a century ago, women participated only rarely in this ritual, and then only if they came from upper-class families. In the nineteenth century, when the greatest part of the population consisted of workers, a great deal was drunk by the 'lower' classes. Wages were paid out on Saturday afternoons in cafés and public drunkenness on Sunday was a common sight. On the following day, 'blue Monday', little work

Like many others, this home was renovated in the 1970s. The furnishings – with heavy sofa combination – are still representative of a large sector of the population.

Insight Holland

Households such as Jan Steen portrayed them may well have appeared romantic, but the present-day Dutch prefer their modern comfort.

At home most Dutch still tend to eat simply. This is not to say that the average Dutch housewifes dislikes cooking, but she will prefer to preserve her best efforts for special occasions. Then a vegetable soup may be made, and a large 'rollade' (a seasoned meat roll of pork or beef) prepared. The specialty of vegetable soup, aside from the different fresh vegetables, of course, is the small hamburger balls that go in it. This is no cookbook, but here is the recipe for those small soup

was accomplished. One of the worst side effects of prosperity is the excessive use of alcohol. More is drunk now on a per capita basis than at the end of the nineteenth century. The problems of alcohol abuse are much greater than those of all drugs combined. But alcohol is socially acceptable, is almost socially obligated. Anyone who doesn't drink at least a little is not quite right.

Dutch emigrants who come back for a family visit do not always have to feel disappointed in their memories of delicious, old-fashioned Dutch meals. 'Hutspot', the mashed carrot, onion and potato pot with sliced beef, is still prepared sometimes, chick peas with fried pork, bean soup with pork ribs, and certainly also the occasional 'Sauerkraut' with Gelderland smoked sausage. But the chance is greater that they will find spaghetti on the table, a Mexican concoction, or Indonesian fried rice with a shrimp cracker.

Dutch food has become very international, and in a comparatively short time. As late as 1950 Austrian and Swiss boarding-house proprietors could not get their Dutch vacationers to eat anything other than Dutch meals. Standard was: peas, fried potatoes and beefsteak. An acceptable alternative was: red cabbage with mashed potatoes and pork chops. When the Dutch began exploring less readily accessible regions in their cars, they also discovered foreign cuisine. For those with more money in particular, preparing unusual foreign meals at home became more than just a pleasant diversion: it was a rage. Talking about food was very important. Traveling to distant places meant telling many stories about food. Many ordinary young Dutchmen also traveled far afield as soldiers, to Indonesia where the Netherlands sat deep in problems. Until before the second world war Indonesia was known as the 'Netherlands East Indies', and it formed a colonial part of the Kingdom of the Netherlands. After 1945 the Indonesians rightly sought their own political freedom. There followed what could be regarded as spontaneous 'wars', which the Dutch euphemistically termed 'police actions', for shame leads to hypocrisy. It was all over the heads of those provincial Dutch boys, who in the meantime had learned to love the country, the girls, and the spicy food – especially that one gargantuan meal: Rice Table, capital letters intended. Our 'typical' Dutch family might eat something like a mashed vegetable pot of endive with meat balls, particularly if the parents were planning on going out that evening and wanted something quick and simple. A fast trip to the greengrocer's on the corner for already prepared endive and potatoes, added to some left-over frozen hamburger balls back home, and the meal is ready. Social visits, particularly for family occasions, are still an important part of Dutch life. A birthday, for example, cannot be missed.

70

balls (about the thickness of the upper knuckle of the little finger) anyway, since they are unknown in many countries. Use lean ground meat, preferably finely-ground veal. Prepare it with egg and soaked bread, bread crumbs, or crackers, and mix salt, pepper and especially nutmeg through it. Form balls and let these cook with the soup for the last ten minutes.

Take a stroll along an ordinary street in a village or town and everywhere you will see well-tended plants on the window sills.

The Dutch are not a very mobile people. Perhaps because of the fastness with which they cling to home life, they are reluctant to move. They tend to regard their home as their home for life. If a large company or government institution contemplates a move requiring a mass relocation of employees to another city, strong protests will be heard, also from the unions. In spite of this, there has been much internal migration in the Netherlands. Housing conditions and work requirements have resulted in the scattering of many families – not only in the last hundred years, with the great trek from the countryside to the cities, but also after the second world war. In the tiny Netherlands, with its quickly coverable distances, the car has proved a blessing for maintaining traditional family ties. The importance of the birthday has also made a contribution to this. The expression 'talking about cows and calves' dates from the time that the Netherlands was still a

Dutch propriety is hard to find on the streets. Clear protests indicate where dogs should do their duty: 'Dogs in the gutter.'

The holy Saint Nicholas did indeed exist, in the city of Myra in Asia Minor, in the 4th century. According to the legend he saved many children from the butcher's knife: In times of famine they were used to supplement the menu. In addition to children, he was also the guardian spirit of merchants and sailors. Italian seafarers even brought his body to Bari after the city of Myra fell into the hands of the advancing Mohammedans. From Bari the St. Nicholas cult spread over the port cities on the Atlantic Ocean and the North Sea. Everywhere St. Nicholas churches were built in his honor. In the Netherlands 23 were erected in the twelfth and thirteenth centuries alone. In the nineteenth century such a church was built in the Amsterdam harbor area. It can be found not far from the Central Station.

land of farmers. Nowadays people discuss pets and houseplants. For these are – after sports – the two major subjects of conversation. Maybe because there is so little nature left outdoors in the Netherlands, people have tried to bring it inside: it is remarkable how many flowers and plants the Dutch have in their homes. This can become a major problem during vacations. Who will take care of them? The same question also applies to the many pets. Kennels also flourish in the Netherlands, not only during the summer vacation months, but also during the winter skiing vacation. What does this in fact mean, all those housepets, those cats, dogs, guinea pigs, rabbits on the balcony, all those tropical fish in the big aquariums? It has much to do with a feeling for warmth and intimacy, and maybe also with 'doing something' for nature: the decline in children is matched by the increase in pets. The possession of animals has no functional purpose, not even that of dogs, for they are seldom watchdogs. A certain practical value can be ascribed to the large aquariums, for they are often harmoniously built into the interior and form – with their green illumination – part of a decorative whole. The aquarium as part of the interior decoration is very Dutch. After their birthday party, our typical couple will make their way home again. Probably one will have refrained from drinking in order to drive. The Dutch law is strict on this point and the police make frequent spot checks. Underway they may discuss family finances, another favorite subject. Perhaps the necessary purchases that can't be put off any longer, and those that can be delayed until the great day of 'Sinterklaas'. This is a singularly typical Dutch celebration, which take place on December 5th, and in fact for weeks earlier. It is also celebrated, in different form, here and there in Belgian Flanders and in Luxemburg, as well as on the Dutch island of Ameland, where the Saint Nicholas feast is celebrated on other days. For the rest the celebration has the same character in all the eleven provinces, whether catholic or protestant: that of an intimate, and rather exuberant family celebration. The present Dutch family celebration of 'Sinterklaas' – or the Good Saint – has practically no religious overtones. The Saint is a kind giver of gifts who rides over the rooftops on a white horse as a descendant of Germanic gods, accompanied by Black Pete, a negro servant who has a somewhat devilish nature but who is also somewhat of an avenger of evil. In the name of 'Sinterklaas' the Dutch give each other an abundance of presents on the eve of the holy day. The gifts are placed in a large basket and everyone pretends they have been brought by the Saint. For this reason they are placed by the chimney, if there still is one. Another tactic is to set the basket on the porch and let a neighbor ring the bell at an agreed time. The entire

Muisjes form a chapter apart. A kernel of aniseed is covered with a hardened layer of melted colored sugar. The crunchy white and red kernels should be eaten on a cracker. A cracker with muisjes is not so much eaten as part of the daily breakfast, but as a festive snack at the office, school or factory, where they are handed around by the proud father or mother of a new offspring. It is thus a sort of birthday treat. If the birth of a royal child is being celebrated, the muisjes are colored orange. Finally, some good advice: spread the crackers generously with butter – otherwise the muisjes will roll off.

The birthday is the most important day in the life of every Dutch man and woman. It is a festive occasion that is celebrated from early until late, at school, at the office, or in the factory. The celebrant distributes treats, chocolates at school, pastries in the office. Presents are given by colleagues and close relatives and friends who drop by. It is not unusual to have thirty of more guests arriving in the evening – in the living room, open and exposed to the entire neighborhood, for the overcurtains are naturally left open. Pastries and drinks are served. Such an evening manifests the comfortable good life, the particularly Dutch kind of intimate conviviality that can only be fully expressed by the word 'gezelligheid'.

celebration takes place under the motto expressed in a traditional song: 'Whoever is good gets treats, whoever is bad, a bundle of sticks.' Weeks ahead the young children may put out their shoe before going to bed, close to the chimney with hay and a carrot for the horse. The following morning they will find the Saint's answer in the form of a bag of candy, but also sometimes a bag of salt, as a warning: be good, try harder to be your best. The real bogeyman is Black Pete, who takes naughty children to Spain, or spanks them with a rod. The celebration thus has a strong moral undertone, which is also apparent from the teasing poems which are supposed to accompany each gift. They are supposed to be read aloud before everyone: the victim is thus made fun of a little. That still fits well in the modern Netherlands. The often extreme surfeit of large and small presents – sometimes little more than gift-wrapped jokes – fits less well in that image. But the adults also give each other household items, or practical gifts, things that were already long needed, on the eve of 'Sinterklaas'. This practical, thrifty policy again fits quite well into the Dutch pattern.

It is a national holiday that is celebrated nationally with a television broadcast of the Saint's arrival from Spain by steamer, and with a procession of the holy man on his white horse through the capital. Shortly thereafter every large store has its own saint. All of those Saints can make it hard on mothers shopping with young ones, but no one minds a white lie more or less in this time. It is a time of sweet deception and fantasy. This Dutch 'Sinterklaas' feast thus differs sharply from the Christmas feast, which is also certainly celebrated in the Netherlands, but with a limited number of gifts. The Christmas tree is the centerpiece of this celebration, the focus of the special atmosphere and of the knowledge that New Year's Eve is in sight. We will deal with that in the following chapter.

Insight Holland

With prosperity comes a new leisure

Insight Holland

Do the Dutch still work eight hours a day, sleep eight hours and have eight hours of leisure time over?

The borders between worktime and leisure time are fading. Leisure is regarded less and less as a reward for labor. Leisure time no longer derives its value from work but has acquired a value in its own right. A well known example is do-it-yourself projects. A better example: so-called volunteer work, which is found in the areas of public recreation (recreational work) nature and landscaping (volunteer landscape management) and sport. In the Netherlands there are more than a half million volunteers active in directing the activities of approximately four million organized sporting enthusiasts. If you stop to think that there are only fourteen million residents in the Netherlands, then this becomes a surprising figure.

Soccer is undoubtedly the most popular sport, enjoying the greatest number of players and spectators. The Royal Netherlands Football League has about one million members and is the largest sporting organization in the Netherlands. But all of the other sports are important, too. In many families the weekend schedule includes set times for playing at one sport or another. Swimming, volleyball, handball, or korfball, not to mention track-sports and gymnastics. Tennis in the warmer months, jogging and later on, after the summer, training for the ski season. The Dutch are enormously active in their leisure time. In general it can be said that the Dutch, particularly those with older children, use and organize their free time very well. A very large part of the population is devoted to being active in a very healthy way. This phenomenon is a direct result of the great increase in prosperity. In the difficult century that preceded this one the great mass of people were much less well off. We quote a Dutch author writing about work and leisure time in around 1880. 'Around the time that the factory shifts changed, the barkeeper set the genever glasses on the bar. The workers stamped in shortly thereafter, not saying a word. They tipped their caps, emptied their glasses, wetting their palates ardently and swallowing greedily. They were already reaching for their next glass. This was emptied somewhat more carefully. A gray and shabby folk was standing around the bar – pale, stooped, deflated men with hollow eyes which showed no spark as they finished off the third or fourth mumbled order. Their large number was matched by the somber fury with which they drank. They would be there tomorrow and the day after. At the end of the week when they had received their wages they would have one extra drink and cursing they would pay their bill for the last seven days. Many were absent from work on Monday, reeking of liquor and snoring as they slept off their drunkeness.' Undoubtedly, the biggest weapon in the battle against the cafe as a pastime has been sports and in particular soccer. This was introduced in the Netherlands in 1879 by the English, but not in an organized context. A lot of British worked in the Netherlands at that time, many as mechanical engineers, helping to build locks, canals, railways and factories with steam engines. In their free time they liked to play football, as they called it. A young man from Haarlem saw this sport and he set up a famous club – HFC, the Haarlem Football Club – with some of his school friends. This was a club for young men from the higher echelons of society. Other clubs were started along the same lines; a league was begun in 1889 and in 1895 this was renamed the Netherlands Football League, which in 1929 acquired the title Royal – The Royal Netherlands Football League (KNVB). It still exists today. Despite a rather fast growth in its first years, it wasn't all easy sailing for the football league. It took a long time before those who were better off allowed their sport to move on to the villages and working class neighborhoods. By the time of the first world war, soccer had become more or less a popular sport. But, the religious elements objected to soccer being played on Sunday and at the same time they were of the opinion that all forms of physical recreation were suspect and could better be played within one's own circle under the supervision of a spiritual advisor.

The Roman Catholic League set up in 1916 formed the beginning of a split that was not abandoned until 1940. In the meantime the sport had become extraordinarily popular both as a participatory and a spectator sport. A number of things contributed to this: a 48 hour working week, an awareness among the workers of the benefits of fresh air, the outdoors and physical activity, and furthermore the spread of radio, which among other things turned the matches between the Netherlands and Belgium into major

The ninth Olympic Games were held in 1928 in Amsterdam, for which a stadium was built on the southern edge of the city.

events in just about every Dutchman's living room. Also the Olympics, held in Amsterdam in 1928 were a major event. In one part of southern Amsterdam the impact of this can still be felt: in the modern neighborhoods with the Greek street names and in the progressive design of the Olympic Stadium that still serves so well today.

After the second world war the interest in Dutch soccer rose enormously. The KNVB, originally a purely amateur club, was forced to start a professional league by the changing circumstances. This move resulted in an improvement in the level of soccer being played in the Netherlands because players who had gone abroad to play professionally could now return and young talent also remained in the country. The financial problems were helped by the sport totalizator: a large part of the lottery earnings are given to the many amateur clubs. Soccer has become so extremely important in the lives of the Dutch that it dominates the Monday morning office and factory conversation. Anyone who can't follow the discussions at least a little is placing himself beyond the national cultural boundaries. On evenings when important national competitions are being broadcast on television the streets of Dutch cities are virtually empty.

A second important development in the field of sports is cycling. The Dutch distinguish between 'fietsen', when referring to cycling as means of transport and casual recreation, and 'wielrennen' when referring to organized racing competitions. The *bicycle* played an important role in the development of the Netherlands and it remains an important form of transportation. The Netherlands has the greatest per capita number of bicycles in the world. There are nine million for fourteen million inhabitants. When in around 1890 the bicycle became affordable for laborers, it began to play a principle role in the industrialization of the farming and village populations, which could now seek work in the distant factories. But, it was also used by country and city doctors, butcher's boys, notary publics, biologists working in the field, school children and the queen. A bicycle was and is as common as a pair of shoes in the Netherlands. In 1883 there was already a bicycle league, which would be called the 'Common' (in the sense of unrestricted membership) Netherlands Cyclists' Association. Fifty years later this would also acquire the title Royal. The ANWB, comparable to the American AAA, has done a great deal for road users. The first activities were concentrated on the creation of paved cycle paths. In 1894 the first road signs, now numbering somewhere around 50,000, were posted.

Although the Dutch have always walked a lot – also as a form of recreation – the outdoors, the discovery of nature, only became popular through the pioneering work of the ANWB, which right from the beginning chose for an educational role with slogans such as a ponderous, if unambiguous rhyme that wagged a chastising finger at would-be naughty campers while reminding them not to thank the local landowner for the kind use of his property by leaving their litter behind on it. Camping, which had already become a popular pastime before the first world war, would never have achieved such a level of popularity without the bicycle. After almost a century in virtually unchanged form, the bicycle remains important for Dutch recreation. Bicycling as a pure sport falls into that category. Competition bicycling is a very important professional sport, although there are still many amateur competitions held. The ANWB resisted the professionalizing of cycling for as long as it could, but in 1896 a Dutchman obtained permission to compete professionally. Right from the beginning

Cycle racing has an undiminishing popularity. Many competitions are sponsored by business.

there were different categories, track competitions and road competitions. In the first category the so-called six day competitions were very popular with the general public. Under the road competitions the marathon Tour de France became the best known. This gruelling contest through France owes its popularity and its importance for large sectors of the population primarily to the mass media. This is also true for a comparable skating competition, one of the most common Dutch sporting events – the 'eleven cities' tour. Skating is very old in the Netherlands, probably as old as winter and ice. In the Frisian 'terpen', artificial hills built as protection against the water, bone skates dating from the beginning of the christian era have been found. What is certain is that skating has been popular in large parts of western Europe since the Middle Ages. Dutch paintings portray an array of wintertime scenes with skaters. The party atmosphere which one feels from such a scene is repeated in the same fashion in our modern time as soon as it becomes cold enough for the waters to freeze solid. Then suddenly all of the country is on skates and sometimes schools are closed. Skating is one of the most common forms of recreation known in the Netherlands. And suddenly there are skating competitions everywhere. Friesland has the honor of having organized the first skating race; that was around 1800. Reports about the Eleven Cities competition appeared in 1809 when two persistent Frisians skated through all of the cities in Friesland in 14½ hours. That was possible in that countryside of water, via the canals. When a non-Frisian Dutchman repeated the feat in 1890, the Frisians felt their honor had been challenged and on Saturday, January 2nd, 1909, the first large-scale Eleven Cities competition was held. Since that time many Eleven Cities races have taken place, especially after the second world war when television coverage of the race made it into a national event, also increasing the number of participants. There were, for example, 10,000 in 1963. That was a difficult year, when only a tiny number of the competition skaters and a fraction of the other participants made it to the finish line. The question now is whether the Netherlands will ever see such a beautiful and awful match again. The water is so polluted that it no longer freezes as easily, and moreover the winters are not as severe as previously. Because of this alternative Eleven Cities competitions have been organized in colder countries such as Finland and Canada. But the Frisians continue to remain prepared. As soon as it even starts to freeze shipping on the route is forbidden. The Netherlands is more fortunate with another national sport, swimming. The Netherlands has had a few very long, almost sub-tropical sunny spells in the last years. One can assume that there have been swimmers throughout the history

The Leidseplein in Amsterdam: in the summer a pleasant terrace under the trees, in the winter an excellent little skating rink.

of the watery Netherlands – only during the warm months, of course, and perhaps not so much during different periods.

Right up into this century swimmers have posed a problem in certain provinces because of their exposed physical appearance. This problem was fought out on two fronts: in the public swimming pools and at the seaside. We find the following written about bathing – and we're not even talking about swimming: 'In the first half of the 18th century there were flourishing seaside resorts with beaches and changing wagons. One descended the ladder to a safe depth, every man for himself. One wore an elaborate bathing costume which covered the body from the ankles to the shoulders. It was perhaps not so flattering, but it didn't expose much of the body and one didn't attract any attention on the beach. That would have been immodest. Only around the first world war were bathing suits designed which allowed for more freedom of movement.' When did swimming become a sport? At approximately the same time as the rise of the seaside pool. As was the case with so many sports, England was the forerunner: in 1834 Liverpool built the first covered swimming pool. A national swimming league was created in England in 1869. But, one year later the Netherlands followed by founding the Amsterdam Swimming League – which has had the royal title since 1933. Then the rage started. Despite the crisis swimming pools were built everywhere. Outdoor pools, pools with beaches in the middle of the countryside, and many indoor swimming pools. Also, many people swam in safe areas at the seaside. Swimming became a popular sport thanks to the continual publicity that the competition sports received during their heyday, such as during the Olympics in 1928 in Amsterdam and in 1932 in Los Angeles. One of the competitors there, Johnny Weismuller, would make swimming even more popular with his Tarzan films. Swimming has had a big influence on personal hygiene, body care, and a freer attitude towards life. But, that is a chapter apart. There is almost no other country in the world with as much water as the Netherlands has and therefore no country where the chance of drowning is so great. That is why swimming is taught in the physical education classes in primary school. Earning an official swimming diploma is a landmark in the life of a Dutch child. Usually there's a party at home after the diploma has been handed out at the swimming pool. Is there a connection between swimming's popularity and the spread of nudist beaches? Perhaps it has something to do with the relatively small number of hours of sunshine and the desire of the Dutch to catch as many rays of sunshine as possible.

Is the primary goal on these sunny days to stretch out at the waterside? Nothing could be less true! There are many active water

Scheveningen, the nationally known and much-sung resort near The Hague.

sports in the Netherlands and these are played by thousands, hundreds of thousands of people. We begin with the latest sort of sailing sport, windsurfing, not because windsurfing is exclusively Dutch – although just about the best surfboards in the world are manufactured in Dutch factories – but because it has so many typically Dutch aspects to it. Anyone traveling anywhere through the Low Countries in the summer will be amazed by the myriads of windsurfers found even on a pond no larger than a saucer. Anywhere there's water, on the first bearable day of the year, people in their black rubber suits – necessary for many months to protect the body against the cold – appear. Windsurfing owes its (all too great) popularity to the wish of all the Dutch to participate in watersports. Up until the second world war it was impossible for a typical working class family to maintain a sailboat. Sailing was for the well to do. It was difficult even to own a canoe be-

81

Insight Holland

cause that had to be kept somewhere and that costs money. The possession of a car and the development of new light materials have helped the surfboard's popularity. Every automobile owner can now take his surfboard wherever there is water, which has also helped to make it an omnipresent, overcrowding public nuisance for many other water enthusiasts. The increasing number of pleasure craft has led to a shortage of space even in this water-abundant land, and to serious damage of the environment from water pollution, noise pollution and destruction of the shoreline. The government is carefully considering how the water areas should be used. The protection of nature, the drinking water supply and shipping all have to be taken into account. Sailing developed during the Golden Age when races were held by the rich on many lakes and inland waterways. It took a long time before this sport lost its elite character and the boat owners stopped feeling too superior to form associations. In 1890 an overall organization was formed. This grew into what is known today as the Royal Netherlands Watersport League. One does not necessarily have to be a member of an organization in order to be able to sail and one doesn't even have to own a boat. There are usually boats for rent at the harbors. Those who wish to rent a boat are advised to reserve beforehand, especially on a weekend. So much sailing is done then that the trick has become not so much sailing as avoiding the other sailboats. Why don't all those sailboats just go out into the North Sea? Because the Dutch coastline lacks natural harbors as well as yachting harbors where one can retreat to in bad weather. Ocean sailing is however undertaken on the North Sea by very large, entirely seaworthy craft, but only a happy few can permit themselves the luxury of such yachts. The North Sea is also not suitable for small motor launches. It is the increase of this type of boat that has greatly added to the recreational pressure on the inland waterways. All of the unbelievably numerous motorboats together have been responsible for serious pollution resulting in a decline of the numbers of plants and animals. Even so, the possession of a cruiser – a floating mobile home suitable for longer journeys – is such a cherished ideal for the Dutch that any restrictive measures would result in major, almost political consequences. A different interest – the underwater sport – was actually able to contribute to the political pressure in the 1970s that influenced the final design of a very important engineering project: the Oosterschelde open dam. Amateur divers had discovered such beautiful flora and fauna there that they joined together with other groups to lobby against making the basin into a fresh water area. More about that in the next chapter. Anyone standing at the shore of a Dutch lake, observing all the motorboats, sailboats, the divers here and there, and especially the innumerable windsurfers everywhere with their colorful suits, surfboards and sails, is a far cry from the atmosphere of the worker as a barfly, as quoted at the beginning of this chapter.

Does this mean that there are hardly any cafes in the Netherlands? Certainly not. The cafe as a place to relax is catching on everywhere, especially in the old neighborhoods and in the centers of large cities. Especially the so-called 'brown' cafes – named for their dark, old-fashioned interiors – are still popular, although more modern stylish cafes appealing to particular groups have also caught on in the last years. Such groups tend to change cafes with the seasons as a way of preserving their exclusivity. In contrast the opposite principle rules in the old familiar neighborhood cafe. The neighborhood and loyalty to it are what is important. These cafes are public living rooms, with the cafe proprieter ideally the friend and advisor of his customers. Many clubs also meet in these places: card clubs, billiards clubs, but also fishing clubs and even pigeon fanciers clubs. First, fishing, to round off the subject of water sports. Fishing is a true folk sport. In the Netherlands it has always been so since hunting was reserved for gentlemen, who left fishing to the lesser folk. But nowadays everyone in the Netherlands fishes, whatever his background, and this sport is probably the most popular form of outdoor recreation. There are approximately 1.5 million fishermen in the Netherlands. On average they each go fishing about 40 times a year. Without stimulating and conservation measures the fish population in the Netherlands would already have been decimated as a result of the excessive use of Dutch waters and the pollution. But the Dutch government has done much to aid sport fishing in the last years. Along with simplifying fishing regulations and making new fishing waters and opportunities available, the most important contribution of the government has been the buying out of the commercial fishers. These had the sole fishing rights to many areas. The aim was to leave the commercial fishers only with the rights to the economically valuable eel. Subsidies were made available for buying these fishermen out. There are many fishing clubs in the Netherlands, most of which are only active locally and hold exclusive rights to one or more fishing areas. They are associated in the General Netherlands Anglers Association. We mentioned above the pigeon fanciers. This is a somewhat derogatory name for a relatively small group (50,000 in the Netherlands) which holds competitions on the national and international level for homing pigeons. Up to the nineteenth century the homing pigeon was the fastest way of sending messages. Its use declined with the coming of the telegraph. Keeping pigeons then became a sport.

Shortly thereafter they became very popular in Belgium. In the Netherlands the sport is most in vogue in the provinces close to Belgium, but it is also found in most of the others. For a long time the sport blossomed in the working class neighborhoods of the capital, especially in the district known as the Jordaan, a uniquely idiosyncratic part of Amsterdam with a distinctive slang all its own that might be compared with London cockney. The 'duiven-melkers' there are regarded with affection. Sometimes they win lucrative prizes. At least as remarkable for the Netherlands are the activities of a larger group, namely the allotment gardeners. Foreigners traveling by train often wonder what all those little houses surrounded by flowers and plants on the outskirts of cities are. They are the day houses of city dwellers who don't want to lose all contact with nature. Originally, around the turn of the century, these public gardens were used to grow one's own vegetables. Especially during the two world wars the gardens were extraordinarily popular. With increasing prosperity the vegetables made way in many cases for decorative plants. The 'beauty of nature' has become the more important consideration. In the meantime, the expansion of the cities has caused many of the public allotments to lose their battle against time. That does not mean that they belong completely to the past. There are still many allotment complexes and they remain a good safety valve for the shut-in life of the concrete buildings.

Because it is forbidden to live in the garden cottages, which are only intended for day use, caravans have become popular as inexpensive second homes during the past 25 years. They often stand in large caravan parks in woodlands or by the water where they form temporary villages. Sometimes it is only permissible to sleep in them during the summer months since they may not be used as a permanent residence. The semi-immobile standing caravan developed from the touring caravan is popular among the thrifty but homy Dutch for vacation trips abroad. But because it had to be kept somewhere when not in use, people also began staying in them as weekend retreats. That the Dutch like to travel, but like even more to return home, has already been pointed out. The standing caravan is proof that this is indeed true for a large part of the population. One leaves one's city home to go home somewhere else. And it is a complete home down to the Dutch lace, so indispensible in the Netherlands, from which the doll house like transparent curtains are made. Dutch family life goes on here as usual, with visits from relatives and friends arriving from all directions. The second home use of caravans and houseboats has reinforced the recreational character of the Dutch family visit. The automobile, the outstanding road network and the small size

Happy with their second home on wheels, the caravan. Many Dutch spend their weekends and vacations in mobile homes on permanent sites.

of the country have all served to forge the nation more closely together.

The symbol of the impressive network of friends and relations is to be found hanging in every Dutch bathroom: the birthday calendar, a friendly tyrant which takes advantage of those captive moments of undisturbed privacy to remind one of the upcoming birthday of grandma, Pete or Cousin Nel. There are also plenty of other holidays. The high point of the traffic jams usually occurs around Whit Sunday – celebrated in the Netherlands on the Sunday and Monday seven weeks after Easter, also a two-day holiday falling on Sunday and Monday. Easter Monday, but especially the Monday after Whit Sunday, are very popular days for making day trips among the orthodox christian population, who are forbidden to travel on Sundays. Christmas is also celebrated for two days in the Netherlands, on December 25th and 26th. The first day of Christmas has a sacred, introverted family character, even for those who are not religious. The light of the Christmas tree, a reminder of the German 'jaarwende', occupies a central place and is more important than the christmas presents. 'Sinterklaas' has already fulfilled this aspect. The second day of Christmas has a more relaxed character, with family and friends visiting each other. New Year's eve is celebrated at home with one's family and friends. More than the usual amount of eating and drinking takes place. A special sort of pastry cannot be absent: the 'oliebol' or fritter. These can be bought already made at the pastry bakery, but tradition requires that they be made at home. Small balls of thin yeast batter are dropped into a deep pan of hot oil. The crispy but greasy balls puff out to about the size of tennis balls or larger and are served with powdered sugar. After midnight, when the handshaking and kissing are over, the New Year's celebration acquires a carnival-like character and people take to the streets with fireworks and noisemakers or drive around with friends to enjoy the displays. A remarkable phenomenon of the last years is the popularity of the actual Carnival, even among non-catholics. Many people, even in the strongly protestant northern provinces, enjoy taking a few days of their vacation time to become caught up in the festive, frenetic near-madness of the days of unbridled fun preceding the period of fasting. The southern cities of Den Bosch, Breda, Roermond and Maastricht are the most popular centers of the festivities, but there is much celebration everywhere throughout the south. More and more Dutch make a point of including Carnival in their vacation days. The number of Dutch going away for their vacations rose sharply in the 1970s in particular, by 50 to 60%. Many average more than two trips a year, often outside of the Netherlands. In 1977, 1978 and 1979 more

summer vacations were spent outside the country than in it. Although the absolute number of vacations taken in the Netherlands declined in 1977 and 1978, that was not the case in 1979. In the last years the preference for vacations in the country has increased. In comparison to other countries, the Dutch have a large number of vacation days, approximately four weeks in total. These are paid for by the employer. Even more impressive: the Dutch all receive a vacation bonus and it is not mandatory that the bonus actually be used for the vacation. One can – in a manner of speaking – use the money to buy a surfboard with it and use his free time in that way: daytime recreation. Such generous employee benefits are rapidly being eroded by the economic crisis, however, and it remains to be seen what will ultimately survive the present dismantling of the overgenerous system that was built up in more affluent times. It has been calculated that since about the middle of the 1970s nearly 90% of the population spends its free time on outdoor recreational activities in one way or another. Participation in such activities is not the same for all parts of the population. In general the lower income groups, as well as those with only a primary school education and retired people are not represented as strongly. Even so the Dutch cities have exquisite parks, many of which were created in the 19th century like the lovely Vondel Park in Amsterdam.

The elderly receive many reductions: on public transport, on movie tickets, and there are special concerts and theater performances for them. It is often the case that one is only in a position to fully enjoy cultural activities after retirement. As there is an abundance of art and culture in the Netherlands – too much actually for the average citizen to keep up with. Amsterdam especially can be considered a cultural laboratory, with its 'experimental' Mickery Theater – famous the world over – its progressive composers, its active museums, its modern ballet, its many public libraries. Many films are made in the Netherlands too. Some films are also successful outside of the country, such as *Soldier of Orange*. Finally, something about the principle contributor of culture to the whole nation, rich and poor, young and old: the television, which belongs to the viewers through associations of them. Broadcasting time is divided among these associations, no less than eight – three 'popular', two protestant, one catholic, one socialist and one progressive – according to the size of their membership. All of these associations also have a share in the Netherlands Broadcasting Foundation, a cooperative body which is charged with providing technical facilities to all the broadcasters. Broadcasting in the Netherlands is therefore a national and in theory an unusually democratic institution which is

'The National Ballet,' a famed Dutch ballet company during a performance of The Sleeping Beauty, with Alexandra Radius and Henry Jurriëns (middle).

financed by a sort of tax on television and/or radio owners as well as by a restricted amount of advertising. Commercials are only broadcast in separate blocks before and after the news. Programs are therefore not interrupted by commercial breaks. That is true of both Dutch television channels. Which doesn't mean that no other channels have access to Dutch living rooms. Cable television is becoming more widespread and many foreign stations can be received on it. Moreover, because the Netherlands is small, large groups of viewers can receive programs from neighboring countries on their own antennas. Viewers living near the border have the advantage, of course. But tall antennas everywhere can receive many programs, even in the center of the country. These and other developments, especially in satellite broadcasting, will definitely have an effect on the protected, uncompetitive, non-commercial Dutch system. In many circles it is feared that the Dutch will lose control of their own programming. Many feel that would be a pity. For the broadcasting system built up from the separate public associations is one of the strongest symbols of the Dutch national spirit: all want to have their own say but all still work on the solution. It is exactly the same as a Dutch lake in the summer: too crowded, all competing for their own pleasure, but everything controlled by associations and regulations to prevent calamaties and chaos. As they say in the Netherlands: 'Everything works out in the end.'

Always busy with water and land

Insight Holland

The history of the Netherlands as a polder nation is the history of a growing national bond.

The highly industrialized countries, with their continuing advances in technology, transport and energy supply, have also become more and more vulnerable over the last hundred years. A collapsed bridge or a malfunctioning power plant can have direct serious consequences. But no other country is as vulnerable as the Netherlands. It would slowly but surely become one big swamp if there were ever a complete and continuing power failure. At least the western part of the country. For this area lies lower than the Amsterdam watermark, the mean level of the North Sea.

The Netherlands is often seen by foreigners as a country where organizations plays a large, even exaggerated role. One of the historical reasons for this is that the Netherlands itself would not even exist without a perfect organization. The modern, self-maintaining Netherlands began its development as a nation with the establishment of organizations for polder management. That was during the Middle Ages. Only later would these polder organizations join together to form a larger network of communities. The history of the Netherlands as a polder nation is the history of a growing national bond.

Long before the Middle Ages successful attempts to make swampy areas habitable had been undertaken. Monks, who were living together in organized communities, built up the hilly mounds known as *terpen*. A good number could still be seen in Friesland and Groningen until into the last century. Terpen were refuges, raised mounds of earth where the people and their animals could find safety during the highest spring tides. Gradually the terpen began to be connected at various places with dikes. When these dikes eventually joined together to form a single, enclosed area, this came to be referred to as a *polder*. The origin of this word can still be found in the Frisian language: 'polle' or 'pol'. It is something that sticks out above a flat surface. Draining the polder and keeping it from reflooding depended upon self-regulating sluices, an invention which the Egyptians had used. They consisted of two doors, fitted in such a way that the departing water during low tide would push them open, so the flow was unimpeded. But when the water tried to return during high tide the direction and pressure of the flow would hold the doors firmly closed so the water could not re-enter.

As long as things were pretty much left to their own devices in this manner not much organization was needed. But it hardly ever really worked out this way, because the Netherlands has an ocean climate with lots of rainfall. And rain and high tides go together. In such instances the polder would become flooded if nothing was done to prevent it. The next step was the draining of the polders by pumping, at first by hand or with draft animals, later with small windmills. With the introduction of that wooden instrument, the Netherlands became a technological country. And in fact also an organized one. For those windmills cost money, and they required regular maintenance. The polder became in this manner a matter of continuous community responsibility. And because one polder often bordered another, there were interests common to the different communities. This was the beginning of the *waterschap*, the polder management organization responsible for the water level, the improvement of dams, the supervision of the common waterways and the cleaning of waterways and ditches.

Did an organized network of water management then rapidly spread throughout the Low Countries? Far from it. The situation remained unclear and full of paradoxes for a long time. As land was reclaimed with much effort in one place, it would be lost in another – not only through intrusions of the angry sea, but often also because of extensive short-sightedness. Until into the fifteenth

The changing shape of the Netherlands since 500 B.C.

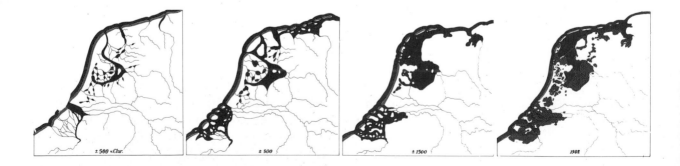

90

century, sometimes even the sixteenth, when there was widespread development, large areas of land were still being lost to the water as a result of poor management of the sea dikes. The image of Hans Brinker, the boy who plugged a leaky dike with his finger, is an American myth, not a Dutch one, but it symbolises very well these contradictory qualities: the courage of a tiny nation against the mighty sea and the clumsiness with which this campaign was sometimes conducted, often piecemeal and haphazard. This was very much the case in Zeeland where peat was commonly dug from the areas outside the dikes. This was done to obtain salt. The peat which was dug up from this land was saturated with salt. By burning the peat, a process known as 'salt burning', the salt residue was left over. In the places where this was done long hills of 'salt ash' could be seen. The Zelke polder near Zierikzee is named after this.

In the fifteenth century this peat burning was repeatedly restricted by ordinance and in 1551 entirely forbidden by Charles v. The import of salt from Spain made the salt burning no longer necessary. In the meantime the damage had been done; entire polders, villages and cities had sunk to below sea level. The decline of the once thriving town of Reimerswaal, for example, was hastened by the excavations beyond the dikes, which removed the land adjacent to them, much reducing their effectiveness. Reimerswaal did not immediately succumb to the great flood of 1530 – the St. Felix flood. The dangerous hole, that had then appeared in the dike close to the city, could have been repaired. But the owner of the polder, a Mr. Lodijke, considered it not worth the trouble. He hated the city, which he regarded as a threat to his own power, and preferred to leave it to the mercy of the sea. In fact, Reimerswaal survived longer than the property of Mr. Lodijke. Every inch of his polders eventually disappeared into the sea, until only Reimerswaal still rose out from the middle of the water, like a ghost town. But life by then had become pointless. Later even impossible. The waves won the battle; gradually the city became a ruin and disappeared into the silt.

Land was also won. That went on continuously. And land was lost, sometimes quickly, in a night, in other cases very gradually. In places this occurred through a series of floodings. That was the case in the swampy area in the middle of the country, where some lakes seemed as big as the sky. The largest of all was the *Flevo* lake, which grew and grew, swallowing up other lakes and finally disappearing itself into the sea, the Southern Sea. That happened after high floods had completely washed the marshy land away. Was this also an instance of human failure? Partially. Certainly there were disagreements in the region. Too little cooperation had been displayed. And too much attention had been concentrated on individual parcels of land. But even with better insight and better organization the technology of that time would have had little effect against the floods. The one of 1287 was the worst. In the night of December 14th no less than 50,000 people along the coasts between Stavoren and the river Eems were drowned. And the new inland sea kept eating away at the land, until the moment – it was around 1300 – that landowners and farmers began building dikes together, wherever it was necessary. But it would not be until very much later that a start would be made on reclaiming the land on the Southern Sea, as lake Flevo came to be known. That project – at least in its entirety – was still too much for the capabilities and knowledge of that time.

Still there are amazing stories to tell of the great efforts and ingenious solutions in the Low Countries of the Middle Ages. For example of the great polder of Waard in the province of South Holland. This was created by damming off the river Maas not far from the sea, and redirecting this to the Rhine. That immense job was completed late in the thirteenth century, and it remains an astonishing question just how that work – with the primitive means of the time – was ever accomplished. Did the champions of this cause overreach themselves in their contest with the water? During one and a half centuries the answer would have had to be no. But when the terrible flood of 1421 came, the destruction everywhere could not be prevented. In the night of November 18th sixty-five villages were swept away. Tens of thousands of men, women and children perished. The very name of the disaster was enough to give the survivors chills: the St. Elizabeth flood, so called because the feast of the saintly Elizabeth of Thuringen would have taken place the following day. An incredibly great deal was lost that night: thriving farms, industrious villages, developing cities. And land, land, land. And the pride in the engineering capabilities. Had everything been only a dream? Not entirely. There is a legend about a child adrift in its cradle, which was kept from capsizing by a cat that held it in balance. The place where it was found is still known as 'Kinderdijk', named for the child. Many more people washed ashore there. In the course of time they established a center of fighters against the sea, dredgers, dike builders, canal diggers, and the like. These tough young men from Sliedrecht later drained numerous lakes – both in and outside of the Netherlands – and they reclaimed large parcels from the Southern Sea. In that area a number of big contracters came into existence, the names of which still live on. They spread the fame of the Netherlands throughout the world with the carrying out of their great hydraulic engineering projects.

The marks in the wall of a farmhouse in Alblasserwaard, South Holland province, show how high the water rose during floods in 1740, 1809 and 1819.

It is a story of gains and losses. In some places land was won from the water, in others it was lost. In the provinces of South Holland and Utrecht, for example, agricultural activities were so intensive that hardly any woodland, and thus fuel, remained. People started to make use of the agriculturally seemingly uninteresting fenlands there. They unscrupulously dug the turf out of the land, which could be used as fuel. As a result of this bodies of water of various sizes, sometimes even reaching the proportions of a real lake, came into existence. In addition, the forces of wind and tides were mainly unimpeded here, so that the water increasingly encroached upon the land. This went on for a long time, and the farmers lost land nearly every year. That resulted in an economic problem, which they resolved by becoming fishers. But a solution in the larger sense this was of course not.

Such a larger sense was sought by Andries Vierlingh, who wrote a famous book in about 1570 in which he made many relevant observations. Vierlingh was a man from Brabant province who knew of the fate of Reimerswaal from his own observations. He was employed by different municipal authorities and he was also responsible for the dikes of an important polder near Steenbergen. Andries Vierlingh was one of the first Dutch water control experts, who made a detailed study of the tides, the formation of silt and sand banks, the strengthening and closing of dikes. Even modern dike builders still occasionally find useful advice in his work *Tractaet van Dyckagie*. Two things stand out. In the first place Vierlingh called for a more professional, and better organized supervision of the dikes. In the second place he advocated an aggressive policy of dike building. He warned against the continuing retreat from the water. His motto was just the opposite: attack. That this advice was followed in the sixteenth century was due to a coincidence of circumstances. Very important was that more money became available and that the value of land reclamation was recognized. Equally important was the technology that was rapidly developing in those years. It was now possible to construct larger windmills with much greater capacity. There was also a remarkable improvement in the pumps. While water could not be raised more than a little over two yards in the beginning,

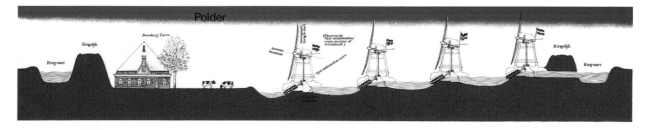

with the new screw-wheel pump this was increased to more than five! Soon these screw-wheel pumps could be seen in many places being driven by – for that time – colossal *windmills*. These ingenious energy collectors were highly popular particularly in the flat, windy region of North Holland known as the Zaanstreek, and not only for keeping the polders dry. They were used for many industrial purposes: sawing wood, grinding grain, preparing paper, pressing oil, shucking rice, and many other kinds of work. By the end of the sixteenth century these industrial mills had become spread throughout the entire Netherlands. Every village had at least one mill to grind the grain of the farmers, particularly after they, through the development of the rotatable cap, could easily be turned into all wind directions.

There were literally tens of thousands of windmills in the Netherlands. Even a century ago, after the industrial revolution had also reached the Netherlands, there were still 11,000 in service. Have they all gone with the winds of time? Fortunately not. A good thousand still remain as monuments; three hundred of these are still in normal use for a number of purposes, agricultural or commercial. The visitor can still see how life in the Netherlands in earlier centuries was conducted; how land was kept dry and reclaimed. This really got underway in the beginning of the seventeenth century, and here we must mention Jan Adriaanszoon Leeghwater, a carpenter and designer, but also a typical renaissance man. This self-taught man did everything. He made clockworks and carillons, tinkered with diving apparatus, built the beautiful town hall of De Rijp in 1530 (still standing there today) and he provided services to the Republic of the Low Countries for important military actions. Finally, he also wrote books, of which the *Haarlemmermeer-Boeck* is the most important. We shall discover why it managed no less than seventeen printings over a number of centuries!

If the Dutch had only dared to drain small and shallow ponds prior to their battle with the Spanish, such as the Dregmeer in 1542 which they began with, now the time had come to start on the larger bodies. For there was sufficient expertise and technical ingenuity available, sufficient organizational interest, and above all, sufficient money. With the shipping and the commerce in tropical waters great wealth was accumulated. A great blossoming was beginning.

Dirck van Oss, leader of the United East India Company and already used to taking chances for the sake of profits, now sought his fortune closer to home. He wanted to invest in the Netherlands. Van Oss cast his eye on a large lake called the Beemster, a worthless body that he was able to buy for a song. Could

Leeghwater perhaps create dry and valuable land there? Jan Adriaanszoon, an entrepreneur to his bones, did not have to be asked that twice. Between 1608 and 1610 he had the lake diked in and surrounded by no less than forty large windmills! It was an undertaking that became a topic of discussion in distant lands, for never had anything like it been seen. The Beemster dried up in 1612. In the meantime work had already begun on the Purmer lake, which became dry in the same year. In 1625 followed the Hugowaard, in 1626 the Wijde Wormer, in 1636 the Schermer. As the years went by Jan Andriaanszoon's fame grew greater and his original honorary nickname ('Leeghwater' = 'drainer') became the name under which he was known and feted abroad. Leeghwater was invited to France, England, Denmark, Prussia and Belgium.

The greatest dream, the draining of a lake in the middle of the land between Haarlem, Leiden and Amsterdam, was not realized. It was Lake Haarlem, about which Leeghwater had written in his book. It was a lake that grew and grew. Sometimes villages and towns seemed in danger of going under. Leeghwater wanted to pump the lake dry with 160 gigantic windmills. Was there a limit? In the century of power and wealth and unlimited confidence none dared to start on the draining of the enormous lake. Still experts in both practice and theory believed that Leeghwater's plan, perhaps somewhat altered, could well have succeeded. During a good two centuries after the appearance of the *Haarlemmermeer-Boeck* it was continually read, and prominent engineers submitted a total of fifteen proposals. Not until 1852 did the dream of Leeghwater, and so many others, become reality. But that was after use could be made of steam energy. One of the three pumping stations was rightly named after Leeghwater.

Much had meantime happened in the Netherlands. The once-great prosperity, the dominance on the seas, the control over many colonies: most of this had been lost. The Napoleonic period in particular had brought things to a truly miserable point. Even so, there were also positive aspects to those two centuries. Some progress in the direction of a centralized public works policy had gradually come about. In the eighteenth century the involvement of central authority had mainly limited itself to assistance during disasters. There were always plenty of those. The area of the great rivers in particular was hit every spring by tremendous floods. The consequences were always extremely tragic. The southwest of the country was also often a disaster area. The stricken polders repeatedly called in the help of the region. Finally a regulation for the dikes in Zeeland province was enacted. That was in 1791. This regulation applied to all matters relating to water control and the like. It was thus an overseeing measure. Still only on a provincial level, but this could already be said to be a big step forward. At about the same time the governing bodies of Holland and West Friesland had appointed an inspector general in the area of water control. This was the highly competent hydraulic engineering expert Christiaan Brunings. After just two years he was even able to bring about an international agreement between the king of Prussia and the provinces of Holland and Gelderland. After that Gelderland also began to become active locally; in 1779 it provided 10,000 guilders for repairing the dike near Heteren. The entire water management system was now seen as a vulnerable network. A local breach here could have major consequences for other parts elsewhere in the land. To Brunings belongs the honor of having a major influence on stimulating this central idea in the Dutch water control. He died in 1805 and lies buried in the St. Bavo church in

The Wadden Sea – a shallow, but still dangerous tidal basin between the Wadden Islands and the mainland – is a rich fishing ground that was in fact previously reserved for the exclusive use of commercial fishers. But since the second world war private parties can also hire a fishing vessel – a party boat – and venture far out onto the salt water.

Haarlem. On a memorial stone are engraved the words: 'The Netherlands' counsel and protector against the Rage of the Sea and the Storms.'

Was the water always only an enemy? It was also an eternal friend. As a livelihood to the fishers, for example. And as a cheap means of transport. The slow tow boat on the inland waterways was a popular means of transport; the Netherlands had a finely meshing network of canals throughout the entire country. The tow boat system on this was well organized; foreigners wrote extensively on the perfection of this. After 1839, the first steam train began service in the Netherlands: from Amsterdam to Haarlem. The tow boat system was so good, that perhaps it prevented a more rapid development of the railway.

Was too much attention paid to the past, and not enough to the future in that century? After the Napoleonic time it had become clear that Rotterdam and Amsterdam would have much difficulty regaining their former positions. Their long channels to the North Sea were inadequate. Inadequate solutions were also conceived and carried out: long canals. The one for Amsterdam, the Great North Holland Canal, was completed in 1824. And that for Rotterdam, the Voornse Canal, in 1830. Neither canal was ever satisfactory, for their routes were not only much too long but also too complicated as exits to the sea for large ships. This is not to say that there is anything wrong with canals themselves. In the water control and in the economy of the Netherlands they are very important, even today. Until well into the twentieth century work was still being carried out on the broadening of old canals and even the digging of new canals. For there is no cheaper means of transport than over water. Whoever takes up an observation point somewhere on one of the major shipping channels in the Netherlands – on the Waal at Tiel, for example – will be amazed at the immense traffic of all kinds of ships on the water going east and west. This is the busiest river in the world.

That Rotterdam and Amsterdam were relieved from their critical position so late in the last century has many reasons. What they needed were wide, short canals straight through the dunes to the sea. Not only the technology, but also the money, particularly government money, was lacking for such projects. For this involved the solution of national problems. The greatest difficulty was that the Netherlands was kept occupied during this period by a deep conflict with the Belgian part, which wanted independence. King William I was a wilful man, not exactly a democratic monarch. Just the same he had a number of good insights about the economy of the land. He was an advocate of the railways. He wanted to have the Haarlemmermeer drained. Through the in-

You encounter them everywhere in the waterways, locks to transport boats to a higher or lower water level.

fluence of his regime provincial regions were given better opportunities. All of this did not change the fact that the king had rather rigid ideas: the northern Netherlands must remain predominantly agrarian, and the southern Netherlands predominantly industrial. In 1839, when Belgium became independent, this idea had to be given up, of course. And that was not at all bad for the Netherlands. Affairs began to be put in order. Enough time had been spent looking to the past, and now it was time to prepare city and country for the future. The reclamation enterprises of Van Oss and Leeghwater in the seventeenth century were still completely private operations. When work was finally begun on the Haarlem lake, the national government stood behind this great work. Lake Haarlem was a community undertaking.

At the same time, some things had had to happen before the community became so active. The huge lake had continued to increase in size, and alarms had continued to be raised as villages and cities were threatened. In 1836 the situation was finally recognized by authority as untenable. On November 29th of that year a severe storm from the southwest struck out over the water and many thousands of people along the edge of the lake waited with bated breath. If Leiden and Haarlem had been threatened before, now it was Amsterdam's turn: the water rose here to the city gates. Less than a month later a gigantic storm out of the northwest blew the water inside the walls of Leiden. In spite of all kinds of continuing opposition, things finally started happening; on May 5th, 1840, work on the digging of a ring channel and the development of a ring dike was started at Hillegom.

This method of drainage was already old in principle and in fact was still just as simple. A ring of two dikes was built around the lake, within which a drainage canal, the 'Ringvaart' came. The water from the lake was pumped to the sea via this canal until the polder was dry. After that constant vigilance was necessary to make sure that the land did not again go under: 'pump or drown'. On that adage the entire Netherlands is built. It took five years before the ring dike was ready. Then the first steam pumping station, the Leeghwater, could begin trials. The second, the Lynden, was ready in 1848. And the third, the Cruquius, in 1849. In 1852 the Haarlem lake was dry, twelve years after the start of the project and three years after pumping had begun. Everything had lasted for a long time, the opposition, the financing, and the achievement. One thing was clearly demonstrated: the great potential that lay available in the power of the new steam technology. The only one of the three pumping stations still maintained in its original state is the Cruquius, standing in the immediate surroundings of Heemstede. After eighty years of service it was shut down, new

Driving piles is always necessary in the low parts of the Netherlands with a soft substratum. And here they have long been busy, in every possible way, with earth moving, sand removal, or clay dredging.

techniques had become available. But it has been preserved by the Royal Institute of Engineers and set up as a museum. It is still a technological hit with the many visitors.

The new drainage enterprise led a shaky existence for a long time. It was true that it had come into existence with government money, but the authorities had no wish to exploit it. It would be some time yet before the Dutch government would assume the role of entrepreneur, such as has frequently happened in the twentieth century. In spite of this the Netherlands slowly began to become a new land. A modern constitution was introduced in 1848, and ever more citizens received a voice. More trains, and roads came, new machine factories were established, also in connection with the agricultural development of the Netherlands East Indies, where ever more sugar industry was wanted. The machines were imported from the Netherlands. It was a time filled with uncer-

tainty, in which old and new were mixed together. For many it was difficult to find any perspective on the future. So did the geography teacher P.R. Bos – famed in the Netherlands for his school atlas – write in 1876: 'The Netherlands cannot really be an industrial country, for this two important raw materials are lacking: coal and iron, and business, agriculture and cattle occupy too many minds and hands.'

Time would teach a different lesson. Amsterdam was already breathing more freely; it was finally freed by a short, broad canal directly through the dunes, a major work that was carried out under British supervision with the effort of thousands and thousands of young Dutchmen from the polders, and already with the help of steam equipment. A completely new town planned by the government came into existence: IJmuiden. And there came what – in that time – were the largest sluices in the world. They were built by the Dutch.

Also Dutch was the development and execution of the new canal from Rotterdam directly to the sea: the New Waterway. It was the project of the public works engineer Pieter Caland, who assumed that the tidal ebb and flow would keep the canal deep and broad. That was a miscalculation that he paid for with his job. The New Waterway was in the meantime saved by the steam machine and the invention of the self-load sand extractor. These would make and keep the Rotterdam waters free up to this very day. Not only does pumping have to be always continued in the Netherlands, but also dredging.

Everywhere a new land was being added to, with river bridges, streetcars in the cities and countryside; the Netherlands began to again become a land that its inhabitants could be proud of. It was a good land. But was it a safe land? Had it been sufficiently armed against the force of the water?

Even before the Haarlem lake was drained dry, many Dutch were talking about a much greater project: draining the Southern Sea. Considering that an emergency situation occurred nearly every year on the edge of the sea, and that there were also repeatedly full-scale disasters, it was obvious that many wished to make a definite end to this. Already in the seventeenth century a famous mathematician had been busy with this. In the twelfth volume of his *Wisconstich Filosofisch Bedrijf* Hendrik Stevin proposed in 1667 to link the islands of the Wadden chain together to: 'drive the violence and venom of the North Sea out of the United Netherlands.' His plan was much too bold for that time, but the basic idea remained. Every time the dikes were breached it again dominated conversation. The disaster of 1826 in particular provided material for discussion for many years. A northwestern storm that continued for days drove the water so high that extremely distant coastal areas were flooded. More than eight hundred people were killed. And about 46,000 cattle were drowned.

Many new plans for the draining of the Southern Sea were put to paper. It almost seemed to be a national pastime – in case any of these plans might ever be carried out. But it would have to be a project of very long duration and it would require immense sums from the government. Thus this precarious subject was carefully and elegantly avoided in The Hague. A new phenomenon emerged: the large, well-organized lobby. In 1886 the Southern Sea Association was set up, in which representatives from 6 provinces, 52 towns, 64 water management bodies and 15 associations of all kinds had seats. It was a serious matter for this association, and it hired the services of a skilled man, the engineer Cornelis Lely. He was commissioned to initiate a study into the real possibilities of drainage. Lely's conclusion: it was possible. His solution of the issue rested upon an inspired pencil line: an enclosing dike between Friesland and North Holland, sealing off the Southern Sea (19 miles). This dike would be the main buffer against the sea. The water behind it would then become desaline quite quickly. And in the quiet, fresh water four separate sections could be diked and drained. And this was what in fact occurred, at least nearly. But we shouldn't get ahead of ourselves. Because it would take until 1918 before definite legislation regarding the draining of the Southern Sea would be passed.

That was thus thirty-two years of struggle for the Southern Sea Association. While in that time the great advocate, Cornelis Lely, was even a minister several times! Not until his third term, from 1913 until 1918, did he finally get the wind – literally – behind him. It was again a storm, the one of January 13th, 1916 – in the middle of the first world war, thus, which fortunately passed the mobilised Netherlands by. This storm also continued, as was often the case, to rage for a considerable time. Ever more water was forced from the North Sea into the vulnerable Southern Sea. The water reached the southern banks there and rose and rose. The islands Urk, Schokland and Marken were submerged. On the last island in particular the results were disastrous: wind and water knocked the fishers' huts loose from their poles and most collapsed; a number drifted far from the island. Many considered it a wonder that the death toll here remained limited to sixteen. On the mainland the damage was also extensive. The entire landscape from Amsterdam to Edam, from Zaandam to Purmerend, was under water. It was an unbroken body of water, above which only the roofs of the farmhouses and the tops of the bare trees protruded. It was fortunate that in this time of mobilisation the

During the construction of the Afsluitdijk more than 16 million square feet of 'zink-stukken' (mattresses) were used. A 'zinkstuk' is a large mat of woven willow twigs which is carefully sunk with heavy stones at a point where the bottom must be protected from the eroding effect of the water.

military could be sent in everywhere to protect the threatened areas and to help the victims. It became clear even in The Hague that they had waited long enough. What was the point in massing soldiers along the frontiers if the country could not even be protected from its old arch-enemy, the sea?

Safety alone was not a gauge of Lely's Southern Sea plan. Another was increasing the agricultural area. With the new polders the Netherlands would better be able to support itself. Here, too, time was a factor. The war had created a scarcity of certain goods, and suddenly prospects looked more promising for the future, the distant future, to be sure, but still a realizable one. In 1918, shortly before the ending of the first world war, the legislation was passed. And so the Netherlands began with a new, great spirit directly after the first world war. The laying of the first part of the enclosing dike, or *Afsluitdijk*, began in 1920. It was the part from the mainland of North Holland to the island of Wieringen. At the end of 1925 this was ready and Wieringen was no longer an island. A short time later work was begun on the second, much larger piece, from Wieringen to the coast of Friesland. That part was closed off in 1932 and the closure was a national occasion that filled the newspapers. A year later car traffic over the dike was possible. An enormous work was completed.

It is from that time that the Netherlands has acquired the reputation in other countries as a technological foe of the water. Not only were safety and agriculture served by the Afsluitdijk and the draining of the polders. This also served as 'demonstration' models by which the engineers, the construction companies, the polder youth and the shipbuilding industry soon felt the benefits: Dutch hydraulic engineering expertise became an export item. The first polder, the smallest – the Wieringermeer – became dry in 1930, before the Afsluitdijk was even completed. It was one of the first parcels of land where the concept of 'ruimtelijke ordening', the detailed and integrated planning of land use, could be applied by the authorities on a large scale. What had occurred with the Haarlem lake area would not be repeated here, on the contrary: the settlement of the emerging land was worked out on paper down to the last comma and was carried out by people with a new profession: the planners. Everything was rapidly completed: ultra-modern farm buildings, roads, canals, a waterway network, the villages Wieringerwerf, Slootdorp and Middenmeer. Just a year later, in 1931, the first grain could be harvested. By private farmers, on state land. Certainly it was a technical success. But no less one of community spirit, and of organization and planning.

In 1936, in the middle of the Great Depression thus, work was begun on the second polder, the Noordoost polder. This became dry

102

land in 1942, at the height of the nazi occupation. The Germans regarded it as just a piece of land that might one day be useful for something. Many Dutch, attempting to avoid the forced labor in Germany or sought by the authorities, found a primitive but relatively safe refuge in the new polder. Directly after the war the Dutch made a great success of the polder. Much had been learned from the Wieringermeer and it was attempted to do the job better here, for example by placing more emphasis on recreational use and natural beauty. The sociologists had also acquired other insights. They created a middle-size city, Emmeloord, as a market center, and around that spread a couple of residential areas with a village character. Close to the farms came the residences for agricultural workers. But this arrangement was already outdated within ten years. First by the motor bike, which made greater traveling distance possible. And then by the democratization of car use. The workers no longer needed to live in the countryside at all. And finally the advancing mechanization made the workers no longer necessary. A portion of the workers' homes are now used by city dwellers as second homes, where they can enjoy the fresh air of the countryside. And the planners learned a lesson. The sea can be coped with, technically. But the future? Nothing is more unfathomable than the sea of time. The original intention was carried out with the first two polders. What about the new polder? One has been completed in two phases. This third polder is known as the Flevo polder and still has a strong agrarian emphasis, particularly in the eastern part. But two very large – and still growing – cities lay in the polder which have no direct economic ties with the surrounding agricultural land. Lelystad and Almere with its harbor area have been planned there – ideally central in the land – to relieve the 'Randstad', particularly Amsterdam, of their great overcrowding. They are satellite towns of the capital, but not exclusively, for there are extensive industrial areas reserved for all kinds of businesses. These have already arrived in large numbers. With an eye to the urbanization of the Flevo polder much emphasis has been put on the laying out of parklands and wilderness areas where a rich bird life has established itself. In any case the character of this polder has become very different from what engineer Lely must have imagined.

What about the last polder, the Markerwaard? A large part of the diking in is ready, and it is even possible to drive through the middle of the sea from the old Enkhuizen to the new Lelystad. But the demand for water recreation has grown to such an extent, as we saw in the last chapter, that the retention of every square foot of water is being fought for. Until now the pressure groups have succeeded in preventing the further draining of the Markerwaard.

In total 65 immense pillars will bear the closable Eastern Scheldt Dam. The more than 130-foot high pillars are formed from concrete in the construction pit of the artificial construction island 'Neeltje Jans' and from there brought to their place in the dam by the lifting ship 'Ostrea' (Oyster). Once the row of pillars is in place, they are connected with each other by an additional construction upon them, adding about another 33 feet.

It is said that the water should remain: for the natural beauty, for the fishers, for recreation and for the water supply.

It is good for the Netherlands that it has had a scientific institute since the middle of the last century, which received in 1905 the status of a technical university, and that after the second world war Eindhoven and Enschede also gained technical universities. Without these universities the industrialization and technological development of the Netherlands could not as easily have gone so far. In this connection the Water Flow Laboratories should be mentioned, which can be found in the Noordoost polder but for which the groundwork was already laid in Delft in 1927. The Water Flow Laboratory also has a good name abroad. It has supported the great expertise of the Dutch in the area of water control and helped to create that aura of a people who are ready to tackle any problem.

Here is just one example: Venice. Since the 1920s this lovely city has been increasingly threatened by the water, like a kind of Reimerswaal. In November of 1966 a disasterous flood occurred which left the city more than six feet under water and seriously damaged innumerable works of art. The Dutch were then requested to contribute to a solution of this difficult situation. That was no problem, technically Venice could be saved. However, as long as the decision making process in Venice and Rome continues with the same bureaucratic slowness, the danger of a new catastrophe remains real. That is a good example for comparison with the 'new' Netherlands. In 1953 a huge disaster again found place in the southwestern part of the Low Countries. In this difficult and then still extremely isolated area made up mainly of islands dozens of dikes were destroyed. A portion of the islands returned to the sea. Nearly two thousand people lost their lives. Tens of thousands lost all their worldly goods, and hundreds of thousands had a pessimistic or at best a dim view of the future. The entire land felt a sense of defeat and everyone suffered along with the hourly developments in the disaster area. How could such a disaster have ever occurred, after so much progress? The answer was twofold: First, because of a rare combination of spring tides with a terrible storm, and second, because the necessary safety measures for the area had not been taken far enough. Work had already begun there without much publicity – the new Lake IJssel (Southern Sea) polders were dominating the news – and good work had already been carried out on shortening and strengthening parts of the coastline, such as in Dutch Flanders around the inland waters of De Braakman, which had been closed off and partially diked. More projects were on the drawing boards, but money was the big issue. The Netherlands was in the process of recovering from the war. There was still incredibly much to do.

But now the strength of the small land, and the changes that had taken place since the work of Cornelis Lely for the Southern Sea Association became apparent. Not only did the entire population feel itself involved with the badly hit distant corner of the homeland – big relief collections were organized and thousands of volunteers came from all over – but the government also reacted with unusual speed and efficiency and came up in the shortest possible time with the *Delta Plan* legislation. In that, it was determined that the entire region would be sufficiently protected within a realizable, short time. And in addition that the entire area would be renovated with new roads, canals and with channels for water control. Where possible and desirable land would be re-allotted. And further the Delta area would be incorporated into the overall land use planning of the country. It was desired that this integration process would be carried out in such a way as to retain the special character of the islands as much as possible.

The first, necessary repairs were begun immediately. Now, in this emergency situation, it again became more apparent than ever what a large arsenal of resources the Netherlands had at its disposal: of construction expertise and materials, of skilled people, of the extensive pool of technologists, and of that famed Water Flow Laboratory. For the closing of the huge gaps new techniques were applied: house-high concrete floats – caissons – were sunk in the current channels. This had to occur at just the right moment, at just the right place. By making use of simulations at Delft those actually doing the work could be guided minute by minute.

The first new project in the Delta works was a technical novelty: a movable storm barrier in the Hollandse IJssel near Krimpen. A little over a year after the disaster construction work was begun

New housing construction in Rotterdam, seen from the Wijnhaven.

Insight Holland

and in 1957 the revolutionary project was completed. Now that was doing something! One could speak of a 'new' Netherlands with justification. In the meantime work had already begun on carrying out the Three Islands plan, and on the damming off of the Haringvliet with a colossal system of sluices. There is an exposition building where much can be learned about this project and the Delta plan. Nearly all of this great complex of works can also be seen from close by and that is most certainly worthwhile.

For thirty years the Dutch have been busy in this former island group with the construction of dams, sluices, dikes, roads, bridges, tunnels, canals, and closable water barriers. The last part of the Delta Plan, the closing off of the Oosterschelde, would already have been completed had there not been opposition from the fishing industry, sport fishers, sport sailers, nature lovers and the ecologists. Under their pressure an investigating commission decided that another solution was indeed recommended – a much more expensive one that the Dutch people – the taxpayers – had to accept. The community does respond to dissident voices, if they are loud enough. In other words: a nation is the sum of its opposites. In the vulnerable Netherlands, there is only one way to be Dutch: together with everyone else. Pump or go under!

The pole house of architect Piet Blom, Rotterdam, 1984.

A nation at work

Insight Holland

In spite of all their leisure time and the discussions of reduced working time, the Dutch still regard work as something unmissable.

There is an expression in Dutch that goes: 'He does it with his clogs on,' which has the meaning of he does it at his pleasure. With the rapid increase in the industrialization and urbanization of the Netherlands at the end of the last century came also a certain condescension towards the clog-wearer, the farmer thus. Nowadays there are significantly fewer farmers than previously. And also significantly fewer wooden shoes. But here and there they are still worn. And certainly not only as part of a folkloristic costume, such as in Marken and Volendam. Or in the extreme religious agrarian community of Staphorst. Or in some parts of the region of the Achterhoek and Twente. All kinds of folk dancing groups still clump around on the Netherlands' best-known symbol. A worn-out symbol? Hardly! For practical use the clog stands in harmony next to the rubber boot. Only 6% of the Dutch working population is now still employed in agriculture, horticulture, the cattle and fishing industry, while these sectors employed the overwhelming majority of people in the middle of the last century. After that it began to decline. That was not only due to the attraction of jobs and factories after 1860. Namely, just twenty years later an innovation found place in agriculture, first with the use of artificial fertilizer, then with improved agricultural implements and better water control through drainage and other techniques. Increasingly fewer workers were required by farms. Still the economic picture of the Netherlands continued to be determined by the agricultural and fishing industries for a long time. Industry was then known as the 'secondary' sector, but it continued to grow, also in the crisis years of the 1930s, and especially after the second world war. Industry was then employer number one. But gradually that

The working population is distributed over the different sectors as follows:

Agriculture, fishing, cattle and horticulture	6%
Industry and production of raw materials	21%
Construction and installation companies	10%
Transport, storage and communications	7%
Commerce, cafés, hotels, restaurants, repair businesses	20%
Other businesses and services	22%
Government	14%

Mechanized transport of sugar beets. ▼

changed too and the turning came in 1963; then industry had to give its leading place up to the so-called service sector.

The shifts in the 'production structure' are due in the first place to a general western phenomenon: the movement to a post-industrial society, the welfare state. For the Netherlands special causes have played an additional role; the geographic position in Europe, favorable for transport, commerce, tourism, the service sector, and the lack of major raw material and energy reserves (assuming one overlooks the minor matter of this country's immense gas reserves); because of this heavy industry could not gain a predominant place in the total structure.

Is the Dutch *agrarian sector* of little importance any longer, now, in the 1980s, with so few employees? Absolutely not! In the vulnerable total Dutch economy this sector is still, also for exports, of great significance. Whoever visits the Netherlands, and

The Netherlands is the biggest exporter of agricultural products after the United States, and without dispute the biggest exporter altogether of a large number of special products, such as flowers, vegetables, pork, and eggs and dairy products.

wants to obtain an insight into this sector in a couple of days, should know that agriculture (cash crops) is carried out for the most part on fertile, well-drained sea clay, in the north of the Netherlands, in the former islands of the southwest, in the drained lakes of North and South Holland, and in the new IJsselmeer polders as well as elsewhere. The most cultivated products are potatoes, sugar beets, and grains (also seed grains). In connection with this agricultural industries came into existence: all sugar beets go to the factory. Much earlier when transport was still difficult, there were many small factories in the clay regions. But for more than a quarter-century a strong centralization has taken place. A few large, extremely modern factories are now sufficient to compete with the world market, particularly with the cane sugar producing countries. The potato is also – partially – a processing material for industry, for example for chips, frozen french

Potatoes are a daily part of the main meal. Immense quantities are also processed into chips and french fries.

'Potatoes for sale' – a familiar sight in the Dutch countryside: farmers sell their own produce, such as potatoes, eggs, vegetables and fruit. ▶

111

fries, instant mashed potatoes, etc. Much older is the potato meal industry, which was established in the northeast of the country from about the middle of the last century. Here also were many small factories in the beginning, most of which were naturally located on a canal for the transport of the potatoes and the disposal of water from the factory. In the last ten years in particular a rigorous centralization has taken place.

How about the Dutch *cattle* industry? Whoever is looking for the large farms will have to go to, for example, Friesland or South Holland. In the cattle businesses the main activities are dairy products, the bioindustry, cattle manure, comes in a much lower place. Important export items are the dairy products. Manufacturing industries are of great importance to the Netherlands. Relatively large quantities of butter and cheese are still made locally on the farms, although there are dairy factories throughout the coun-

Dutch cows are excellent milk producers. In the weeks immediately following the birth of young they can produce as much as twenty-five or more quarts a day. On average they deliver 16 quarts daily.

try. Strong concentrations in the dairy industry as well have not been avoidable. Very large companies now manufacture a selection of products, of which pasturized milk for the national daily demand would have to be mentioned first: the Dutch are great milk drinkers. But a portion of the milk is also exported. In the second place would come cheese, not only for the domestic market although much cheese of Dutch manufacture is also consumed in the Netherlands. Export is very important. Many sorts are made, and in many forms. Then comes butter. Very large export products are milk powder and canned condensed milk. Millions of cans go to the Third World. They can be preserved for long periods and can tolerate many climatic conditions. Much research is carried out in the dairy industry. Every drop of 'left-overs' can be made use of, for example by making a soft drink from them. Another example: manufacturing products from whey for use by the pharmaceutical industry and others. Next to the cows on the dairy farms, pigs and poultry are particularly important, especially for so-called factory farming. Pigs, chickens and eggs are produced in the Netherlands under the same laws and requirements as industrial products. The strong advance of the very large cattle feed industry has to do with this. This branch of industry is carried out along strictly scientific lines and regards the informing of this processing industry as one of the most important means of enabling the clients to produce as efficiently as possible. What the above is actually about is to make it clear that the six percent in the agricultural sector have a large industrial back-up: agriculture and cattle form the starting point of the farm as big business. *Horticulture* is mainly concentrated to the south of The Hague, in the Westland. Independent of the weather, production there continues throughout the year in heated greenhouses. A link with tourism can be found in one part of the horticulture industry: the famous bulb production, which is mainly done in the hinterland of the dune area south of Haarlem and including Lisse and Hillegom. Here an agricultural branch helps to form a display for all of the Netherlands. In the spring many thousands come specially to see the wonder of the colorful, blooming bulb fields.

It is now high time to turn to *industry*, which for a long time was employer number one. First a bit of industrial history, very brief, more follows in the next chapter. The Netherlands already had a thriving industry as early as the seventeenth century, primarily a food industry. But there were also others: shipbuilding, brick factories, gunpowder factories. In the nineteenth century new agricultural industries also were added, the dairy industry, potato meal factories, sugar and straw-board factories. The textile industry in the eastern Netherlands emerged. Machine factories slowly began to grow, along with construction sites for the making of bridges, etc. Shipbuilding received a new impulse from the iron hull and the steam machine. At the end of the century the production of electric light bulbs was begun on a large scale in Eindhoven.

As far as energy goes: in the beginning much turf or imported coal was still used in the factories. After the turn of the century the mining of coal, particularly under the influence of the state, began to assume major proportions in the southern Netherlands. Thousands of miners earned their livings there. At the same time, a chemical industry was established here to process the waste, which acquired large dimensions after the second world war and

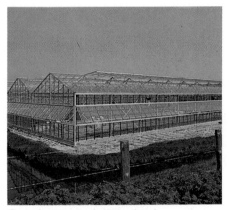

Greenhouses in the Westland.

The surprising growth of Dutch industry can be seen from the following table (in units of volume):

1930	96	1958	204
1938	100	1970	500
1946	47	1977	635

The ferries of the municipal transport authority carry cars, cyclists and pedestrians over the IJ for free.

continued after the mines were no more. Those were closed after mining became unprofitable, particularly in relation to gas, which was found in Groningen from the 1950s onward. The discovery is among the largest in the world. The distribution and winning of this gas required only a few workers and could not absorb the surplus of unemployed in the mining region. It was in this period that industry as a whole – because of extensive mechanisation or the transferring of companies to other countries with cheaper labor forces – lost its first place as an employer. Still thirty percent of the working population was employed in industry (including the construction, installation and agricultural industries). Although the Netherlands production figure has sagged somewhat in recent years, about eighty percent of exports is still made up by Dutch industrial products. Thus, number two as employer still remains number one as exporter.

In the meantime it has already become a bit old-fashioned to make a strict division between the agricultural and industrial sectors. Not only are they largely intermingled, but in addition to that many agricultural enterprises have become industries. It might be better to call them both production industries to emphasize the distinction from the largest (in employees) sector, the so-called service sector.

This *service sector*, which employs 64% of the working population, is much less easy to describe than the other two. There is a paradoxical multiplicity: the medical professions, the social workers, but also the personnel in the hotel, cafe and restaurant businesses, gas stations, repair businesses, further those employed in commerce, transport, storage, communications, the teachers, the civil servants on all levels, and branches of government. The large growth of this service sector is for a large part due to the strong expansion of government involvement in the welfare state, to the demand for more, thus longer, education, to the growth of public health, the interest in the solitary and the aged, and to the bureaucratization of daily life. But it has also grown towards the material side: people go out more, use the car more, watch television more than, say, thirty years ago.

In the beginning of the 1980s we see that of the more than fourteen million Dutch nine million are in the age group between 16 and 65. At sixteen one may work, and at sixty-five one usually has to leave one's regular job. Of the nine million Dutch only five million make up the work force. Of the four million left over, three million are housewives. One million are unable to work as a result of unemployment, illness and permanent disablement. Social legislation for these can still be called relatively good, especially when compared to fifty years ago. Benefits have been

You may live ten floors up in the new residential district of Bijlmermeer, southeast of Amsterdam, but sometimes you still need to be able to play in peace in the sandbox at ground level.

Built-in intimacy of a new residential district in Zoetermeer, South Holland.

This older street in Delft has become a 'residential compound', without cars and dangerous traffic.

Insight Holland

sharply reduced as a result of the recession and much uncertainty currently exists about additional cuts and proposed major changes to the entire welfare system, but at present the overall level of benefits can probably still be termed not unreasonable, and certainly when compared with most other countries. Whoever reaches the age of 65 and has not built up pension rights elsewhere can still count on a state old-age pension. People of this age who wish it can move to a smaller home. Those who already have everything they need, and do not anticipate additional major purchases, can probably still get by on the state old-age pension, although it is becoming increasingly difficult. The elderly are also eligible for various reductions: on public transport, for movie houses, some concerts, and the like. Help is available in the form of social workers and nurses during illness and recovery. Warm meals served at home are available at reasonable prices.

How much do the Dutch pay on average for rent? As little as possible. The Netherlands is traditionally a land of rental dwellings. With government help the rents are kept as low as possible. For this reason it can sometimes happen that those who have advanced in their careers to high salary levels may occupy homes with very low rents. Only for about fifteen years were Dutch rents gradually brought up to the levels in other countries. Whoever pays about a quarter of his income for a good home is paying a reasonable amount by international standards. The Dutch still find that much too high.

All homes with rents below a certain level, which are controlled, are tied to a system of permits. Only those who fulfil certain requirements are authorized to occupy these homes, but there is always a shortage of them. Whoever rents a home above the minimum, but has difficulty meeting the rent, may be eligible for a partial state subsidy.

Whoever has the money is free to buy a home. Many have done that in the last fifteen years, for it seemed reasonable: the interest on the mortgage was tax-deductible. That went fine as long as there was a regular monthly income. Home owners who lose their jobs have tended to fall outside the welfare umbrella, and often end up losing their homes as well.

In spite of the recession there are still significant numbers of people who live in very expensive homes. Because the Netherlands is only a small country and there is nowhere that homes can just be built according to the wishes of the owner, the grand homes that do exist are that much more noticeable. Many Dutch feel that great wealth is unreasonable. The rich have their own opinion about that.

What is the distribution of income like? There have been times in the Netherlands when the highest-paid earned at least fifteen times as much as the lowest-paid. The difference, at least in salaried jobs, is now about five times. And theoretically less. For the highest income categories also have very high taxation rates. An example: someone who earns one hundred thousands guilders a year pays about half on taxes. The net income is about fourty thousand guilders. Many in the lower income categories still find this too high, and of course there are always loopholes when the amount of money involved makes these worth pursuing. There are many in the Netherlands who thus call for a maximum salary limit, but there is no political momentum for this.

There is an official minimum income, although even this is becoming uncertain, at least for younger people. At the beginning of 1984 this was about 1800 guilders a month for those old enough to be officially regarded as deserving full citizenship rights (23); from this the net income retained was about 1400 guilders, approximately $ 450. Taxes are automatically deducted, as well as all kinds of state social insurance premiums, such as for health insurance, social security, and the like.

Is the Netherlands in fact a socialist country? Certainly not in the East European sense of the word. In many respects it might be considered socialist, especially by Americans, but in others it is not. Under the Dutch political system, it is practically inconceivable that any single party could ever win an absolute majority and all governments are necessarily coalitions. The largest socialist party, the Labor Party, has for many years since the war also been one of the largest national parties, occasionally slipping into second place behind the merged confessional parties depending upon momentary political trends, frequently emerging as the biggest for a time. The party has also led or participated in many governments since the war. In general it can be said that a strongly social policy has been carried by all post-war governments, whatever their political leaning, at least until recently. If one takes an historical view, then in terms of practical politics there has not really been all that much difference between the parties, whatever their ideologies. This is probably largely due to the inevitable compromises forced by the coalition system.

Emigration has already been dealt with in a previous chapter. For a long time the government maintained an active, encouraging policy for would-be emigrants without actually promoting emigration as such. There were, however, assistance arrangements for emigrants. For all practical purposes, we are now talking about the past. The waiting lists are long, the requirements high. On the other hand, the desire to emigrate has subsided. The risk is too great: nowhere are the welfare provisions as good as in

Police on horseback escort a demonstration of people seeking a shorter work week at the same pay.

the Netherlands, even today. Another digression in this area: there was also a Dutch 'brain drain'. In the 1950s and 1960s many Dutch technologists departed, mainly for the USA, which was undergoing a boom in that time. This emigration did not only have to do with money, but also with a desire for more space and freedom: the geography and excessive organization of the Netherlands has a claustrophobic effect on some. With the gradual movement towards a European Community and the opening of internal borders to each other's citizens, that feeling has partially subsided. Every Dutch citizen can freely settle and work in every country of the EEC. This can also be seen the other way around, particularly in clinics and hospitals, where many non-Dutch are employed.

In general the urge to come to the Netherlands is much stronger than the urge to leave. For many the Netherlands is, in spite of the structural unemployment, still an ideal country. Those with jobs are in some respects better off than the self-employed, who still have to wade through mountains of official paper in their 'free' time. There are provisions for artists, grants for writers. Actors who find themselves out of work for a time do not necessarily have to become dishwashers immediately thanks to the reasonable unemployment provisions, but this again is rapidly changing. There are still in the Netherlands small entrepreneurs, traders, manufacturers, constructors, builders, exporters and many others who see opportunities to build up larger businesses, in spite of all the obstacles. This even applies to some small farmers who manage to build up their business somewhat to improve their incomes. The point is that the Dutch, in spite of all their leisure time and in spite of all the discussions of reduced working time, still regard work as something unmissable. Now that obtaining work at all seems for many to have become a privilege, it might be suggested – however paradoxical this would appear – that the result in the longer term may be more an enhancement of the quality of life than a diminishment of it. The realization is perhaps growing that a feeling of well-being does not come only from material things. Who does still work, works hard and with a sense of community spirit. What is certain is that he does not do it with a sense of indifference.

The strategic position of the Netherlands in the heart of the EEC is an important contributory factor to the growth of our agrarian trade with other countries. The great significance of the – open – EEC market for our country is apparent from the fact that about 75% of all exported agrarian products are sold there. Of the 'ten', West Germany is by far the largest customer. Agricultural products are also imported on a small scale – in comparison with exports, particularly cattle fodder and raw materials for the food and confectionary industries. A few expressive figures: In 1980 we exported about $10.5 billion worth of processed and unprocessed agricultural products. The 'positive balance' was more than $3 billion. This compensated more than half of the trade deficit from all other products.

Export: the gold in chickens and light-bulbs

Insight Holland

The Netherlands is an exporting nation. But at the same time, it is also a nation that cannot manage without substantial imports.

In recent years imports and exports have more or less balanced out. Sometimes export figures are higher, sometimes imports. This relative equilibrium has not always been the case, and has come about because of the most important Dutch natural resource: natural *gas*. It is a particular blessing for the Netherlands that it can make direct use of this gas itself. And moreover that it can export a considerable portion. The precarious side of this is that it has to do with an insecure item. Demand for it depends greatly on the prosperity at home and abroad. In addition, it cannot be used as a basis forever. Since the discovery of the gas in the late 1950s in the province of Groningen, estimates regarding the total reserves have been revised steadily upwards. The entire country was switched over to gas at a rapid rate, and that brought about a radical change in energy policy. Production was cheaper, which also made export cheaper. Thus the gas itself became an export product. The growth in consumption of gas was so rapid that it was already starting to worry the Dutch at the beginning of the 1970s. In 1972 a supply contract was concluded with Norway. The Dutch government then tried to put a brake on the rate of export somewhat by refusing new contracts. Now, well into the 1980s, much Dutch gas is still being produced, although the recession has reduced demand. Nobody knows for certain how long production can continue. But with some care that will certainly be until the beginning of the twenty-first century.

A much more certain resource for the creation of exports is the soil upon which the Dutch live. We have already seen how difficult and costly it is to keep a large part of that soil dry. And over the past thirty years a substantial part of it has been 'lost' to urban development. This loss has been partially compensated by the re-

Already in antiquity the Chinese and the Egyptians were hatching eggs by incubation. Now that tens of millions of eggs must be hatched annually, this is done on special chick farms. Three weeks after the eggs are placed in the incubator, the chicks emerge.

claimed land in the former Southern Sea.

The *agricultural sectors* are highly developed in the Netherlands. Altogether these usually account for more exports than imports. The export value of all agricultural products, together with those of the fishing industry, is about $ 13 billion. For its small surface area the Netherlands possesses an exceptionally large number of livestock: there are more than five million head of cattle, and more than fourteen million pigs. Also impressive is the amount of poultry. In addition to almost one million turkeys there are over eighty million chickens. The Netherlands is the biggest exporter in the world of chicken, meat and eggs, as well as one of the most important exporters of live chickens. The progression of the Netherlands can be seen from the fact that the poultry stock doubled between 1960 and 1980. With the growth of the poultry stock has also come a considerable decrease in the number of poultry farms. This process of fewer and bigger is due to research and information and a corresponding technical development which has also resulted in an enormous saving of labor. This applies on every level, not only for the farms, but also, for example, for the poultry slaughterhouses and the sales organizations. Taking all this into consideration, it is not surprising that it is precisely the Netherlands where producers of machines and installations for the agricultural industry in all branches have become concentrated. Most of these producers have built up an important export market for their ingenious devices. For those who have a special interest in poultry: as early as 1921 a central institute for poultry research was set up in the Netherlands. This institute, 'Spelderholt' in Beekbergen, employs more than one hundred people and is occupied with many aspects of the poultry industry, from the poultry itself to those who consume it. Spelderholt has many specialized departments where new developments can be tested in practice. One of the latest investigations had to do with a fully automated packing machine for chickens that have to be transported – by plane – abroad as soon as possible.

The same is true of another 'agricultural' product, the cut *flowers* from Aalsmeer. Every visitor will notice how many cut flowers (and potted plants) are bought in the Netherlands in the many shops and street corner stands, and on the markets and even at special flower markets (for example at the Singel in Amsterdam). Rich and poor in the Netherlands have one thing in common: there must be a bunch of fresh flowers in the living room. In comparison with other lands cut flowers are very affordable in the Netherlands. This has to do with the large production. Every visitor can see for himself just how large that production is on any

More than three-quarters of the floral production goes abroad, to the considerable benefit of the Dutch economy. And enough stays behind for the domestic consumer. Flower stalls can be found everywhere.

working day early in the morning, at the famous flower auction in Aalsmeer. The increase in export over the past twenty years is due to the location of Aalsmeer near Schiphol International Airport, home of KLM. It is not surprising that KLM has become a specialist in the rapid transport of fresh-cut Dutch flowers. A substantial part of this trade also goes to the USA nowadays. Dutch horticulture has also been able to improve its export position because of the efficient air transport, especially for longer distances. For shorter distances road transport is still increasing. The most important horticulture products exported are tomatoes, cucumbers and fresh vegetables; they mainly go to West Germany. A special branch of horticulture, the cultivation of flower bulbs, is one of the Netherlands' show pieces: whoever says flower bulbs thinks of the Netherlands. They are exported all over the world, in very many varieties. Whoever wants to see most of these can best go on a spring day to the waving fields of the magnificent 'Keukenhof' park, which is specially devoted to the variegated beauty of Dutch tulip bulbs.

For those who are interested there are more country showcases, cattle markets for instance, of which the most famous are those in Leeuwarden and 's-Hertogenbosch. There are also markets specially for horses, a Dutch export product. A very old market is the one in Zuidlaren in Drenthe, which is held late in the autumn.

Furthermore there is a cheese market every Friday in Alkmaar, a colorful happening where cheese carriers still transport the cheese as it was done centuries ago. It is a tourist event. Here the round little cheeses known as Edam are mainly traded. In one sense the Alkmaar cheese market has long been presenting a distorted image. Not only is Dutch cheese made according to the most modern techniques and with the most modern machinery, it is also traded and distributed according to very efficient methods and exported in huge quantities. The export value is now in the region of $ 700 million. The preceding pages show how one thing leads to another: from agriculture to the factory – even the machine factory – to tourism, also a form of export in a way, export promotion anyway.

Now it is time to make an orderly transition from the farmers and horticulturalists to the exporters of foodstuffs and confectionaries. Most factories in this sector use Dutch raw materials. That is the case, for instance, in thirty industries that work up fish and in only slightly less than thirty that process fruit and vegetables. The *dairy industry* in the meantime forms the most important part of the nutrition industry. There are about 140 milk factories in the hands of 47 enterprises. They process nearly the entire Dutch milk production, which is almost 11½ billion quarts per year. And how important this branch of industry is for Dutch exports is again proven by the following figures. Of the 476 million pounds of butter no less than 600 million pounds are exported, which is to say: the Netherlands still has to buy butter from one country in order to be able to meet its exports to others; more is exported than produced. As for cheese: total production is 1,058 million pounds, of which 699 million are exported. With condensed milk exports are also high: about 1,036 million pounds of the more than 1,235 million are exported. Milk powder production is almost all exported, 818 million pounds. The Netherlands is the biggest exporter of cheese and condensed milk in the world. The products are sold under many names. Often different brand names are used for different markets.

Another export branch of the food industry is formed by *meat* and meat products. The Netherlands has more than 200 export slaugh-

The Dutch cheese assortment is not limited to just the well-known Edam and Gouda cheeses. Other sorts: cream cheese (60%), white spring cheese (48%), Amsterdam cheese (48%), Leiden cheese (40% and 20%), Friesland cheese (40% and 20%), Maasdam cheese (45%), herb cheese (50%), Kernhem cheese (60%), 'pastoral' cheese (40%) and 'farmer's' cheese.

Insight Holland

terhouses that mainly process the meat of domestic livestock, cows and calves, but mainly pigs. Dutch ham is especially in demand. This also has many different brand names. Each year two million tons of meat are processed by this branch of industry.

Now we come to a liquid product, *beer*. Although certain Dutch brands (first Heineken, then Grolsch) have become rather popular abroad in recent years, the Netherlands is a relatively small export nation and even a rather small producing one. The Dutch themselves each drink about 66 quarts a year, half of what their German neighbors consume. From the hundreds of breweries of the past centuries there are still presently fifteen left. Together they produce about 1.3 million quarts. A quarter of that is exported. The large modern firm of Heineken B.V. resulted from a merger of two older breweries in 1968, Amstel (1870) and Heineken (1873). In addition to its European interests the firm has many subsidiaries in developing countries, particularly Suriname, on Curaçao in the Netherlands Antilles and in Africa. The group also has interests in foreign breweries. It is also not limited to just beer, but is active on the market with distilled wines and soft drinks.

To the consumer, anywhere in the world, Heineken is a special name. The thousands of foreign tourists in Amsterdam know immediately where to find the brewery, the address is passed on by word-of-mouth. Why? Because every working day the brewery (on the Stadhouderskade in Amsterdam) offers guided tours with a glass of beer afterwards. Early in the morning there is always a long line of interested people waiting.

A popular strong drink in the Netherlands is *genever*, Dutch gin, which is drunk straight and comes in two varieties: old and young. This no longer has any relation to aging: the old simply has a stronger taste and a somewhat higher alcohol content. In general the taste of genever does not appeal to foreigners very much. Dutch liqueurs are popular abroad, but they are not great buttresses of the export trade.

Well known everywhere is Dutch *chocolate*, a product of an already centuries old and typically Dutch processing industry. There are more than 70 cocoa and chocolate factories in the Netherlands, of which many date from the time of the big windmills. The factories nowadays are ultra-modern, but still work according to the old recipe; import (of cocoa beans and cocoa butter), refine, and export again as much as possible.

The use of cocoa and chocolate in Europe is already more than three hundred years old, and the first western country that occupied itself with production was Spain, the colonizer of Mexico. The Aztecs there had already been growing the venerable beans for many years and knew many things to do with them. The first

Three hundred and fifty-two million quarts of beer (+5.5%) brewed by or under license of Heineken were sold in the western hemisphere in 1982. The greatest concentration of activities was in the export from the Netherlands to the United States and Canada.

public house for chocolate drinking in the Netherlands was established in 1660. The drinking of chocolate became fashionable at that time in Europe, but it was an expensive hobby in the beginning. After the beginning of the 18th century the price fell when the Spanish King sold his monopoly after cocoa had been cultivated in the French, English and Dutch colonies.

The refining of beans is a subtle process for which the Dutch – especially in the Zaanstreek – developed much skill. It was only in the nineteenth century that Dutch cocoa and chocolate acquired special fame. This was due for a large part to the producer Van Houten, who discovered a method of preparation with alkali carbonates that removed the sour taste from the cocoa beans. But there were – and still are – more major brand names, Droste, Bensdorp, Verkade. Many smaller factories went under as the trade in beans, cocoa butter and powder is very concentrated. With 50,000 tons per year the Netherlands is the biggest exporter in the world of cocoa butter and powder, and the main importer of cocoa butter from the producing countries that nowadays are mainly situated in Africa. The most important customer of the Netherlands is West Germany. An important portion of the cocoa powder is exported to the United States.

The history of the economy is also the history of the society. No sector of industry has had an independent development, but rather an interdependent one. For this reason the history of even something as common as margarine can be very fascinating. Called *artificial butter* at first, the product is only just over a century old. It was prepared for the first time in 1869 by the French chemist Hippolyte Mège-Mouriès during a butter shortage in France. Almost immediately – as soon as 1870 – the invention was taken over by two Dutch butter traders, Jurgens and Van den Bergh, who were both located in Oss, a town in the province of North Brabant. That was a center of the pig trade and of the pork processing industry, which included the export of bacon to England among other activities. The superfluous pork fat could be used for the new industry. But right about 1870, as the iron steamship was coming increasingly into use, the trade in vegetable fats from the tropics increased, particularly that of copra (dried coconut). The major margarine and soap producers tried to develop a firm grip on the copra market and acquired interests in plantations. With that they soon achieved an international status. It is obvious that only the biggest could sustain this on the world market. In the 1920s Jurgens and Van den Bergh achieved all kinds of cooperative agreements, not only with each other but also with other enterprises in the field of oils and fats such as Calvé-Delft, and Hartog in Oss, the processer of pork and the founder of Or-

ganon at the beginning of the 1920s when the pancreas waste product could be used for the manufacture of insulin. In 1930 an accord with the soap manufacturer (Sunlight): Lever Brothers resulted in the conglomerate that from then on was known as Unilever. The enterprise now controls 500 companies in 75 countries, where more than 300,000 people are employed altogether. Only six percent of these work in the Netherlands. In turnover Unilever is the twelfth largest enterprise in the world. It is the third biggest in Europe, after British Petroleum – number two – and Shell, another international company that is historically interwoven with the Netherlands. In addition to product groups for foodstuffs and such things as detergents and toilet articles, there are also departments for chemical products, packaging materials, cattle fodder, plantations, fisheries, and transport, including the Norfolk line.

Another small figure to end with, in order to return to our starting point. In the Netherlands there are seventeen margarine factories. Most of these, like so many other companies, belong to Unilever. Such Dutch brand names as Blue Band, Bona, Era, Croma, Calvé, de Betuwe, Iglo, Unox and Zwan are Unilever products. Some of these brands are also sold abroad. This is not to say that they will have been made in the Netherlands. With a conglomerate as big as this one, the national export (and import) figures are not etched too sharply in the economy, to put it obfuscatorily.

The ties with the Dutch colonial past are still clearly visible in the triumvirate *coffee*, *tea* and *tobacco*, which used to form part of the 'colonial goods', as some grocers wrote on their shop windows. Often they are processed within one firm, such as Van Nelle of Rotterdam, Douwe Egberts in Utrecht and Niemeijer in Groningen, although there are also separate companies for the different products. In the tobacco refining industry there are 24 companies in the Netherlands and in addition 16 coffee roasting factories and tea packing houses.

Until 1959 the Netherlands was important in the international tobacco trade and possessed two large auction houses in Amsterdam and Rotterdam (the main receiving harbors), especially for Sumatran and Javanese tobacco. In connection with the poor relations between the Netherlands and Indonesia resulting from a political struggle around New Guinea, the Netherlands then lost the auction rights. These were given to the German city of Bremen, which gratefully made use of them and quickly set up good provisions. The cigarette industry is very internationally oriented. The large companies have separate factories in various countries. The cigar and cut tobacco companies, however, have a more national character although concentrations also occur here. The Dutch cigar industry is already very old and in the early days was spread

In normal years the production of Hoogovens is enormous: almost 4.5 million tons of pig iron, over five million tons of steel, almost 3 million tons of rolled steel products, over 1.25 million tons of steel intermediaries and cast steel products. And on top of that more than half a million tons of coated and uncoated tinned iron.

The Royal Dutch Blast Furnaces and Steel Factories is in fact still a relatively young company. It was established in 1918 at a strategic site, namely at IJmuiden on the North Sea canal and the North Sea. The last, sixth blast furnace from 1967 is the largest in the world and processes 3,000 to 4,000 tons of iron ore.

throughout the entire country; everywhere there were cigar makers together in small companies. The mechanisation of the product has changed that situation drastically. The factory product has a hard time distinguishing itself. Yet the 'Dutch cigar' still has a special attraction in Germany. And in the sector of smoking tobacco the export market – thanks to international campaigns – has actually booked great success over the last few years.

Now we go from food and confectionaries to the *metal industry*, still a big employer in the Netherlands. The Netherlands does not possess usable quantities of iron ore in its soil and the Dutch government therefore decided to build an iron and steel factory at a strategic location, namely at Velzen, on the North Sea channel, near the sea. The iron ore could come from the west by boat and the coal from the east by rail or ship. Since the early 1920s, when Hoogovens began to undergo substantial growth, with many subsidiary opeations, the Netherlands has benefited much from this ultra-modern company. Especially after the second world war it began to take on the function of an economic pillar, an example and a symbol of all of Dutch industry, of the prosperity of the nation. When the prosperity decreased at the end of the 1970s and a world recession announced itself, things did not go well for this Dutch company, in spite of a merger, initially with a German company. The merger turned out to be far from successful and Hoogovens is now no longer a multinational company but a very national one: the Dutch government had to help out with an amount equal to about 500 million dollars. In the beginning of the 1980s dismissals were unavoidable.

The unemployment figure for the Netherlands has risen to well over 800,000 people, that is more than 17% of the working population. 'The high personal and collective living standards, which have been so characteristic of the Netherlands,' wrote the Organization for Economic Cooperation and Development (OECD), 'are being jeopardized by the need to support a rapidly growing portion of people without work.' In the meantime productivity has increased. There is even – not for everyone of course – a certain appreciation of the concept of sobriety. Many people believe that the Netherlands is going through a transitional period and that the conjunctural slump is an opportunity to consider restructuring measures and long-term possibilities. The runner pauses, takes a breather, and tries again to find a new rhythm. That things have not gone badly everywhere in the Netherlands, and have sometimes even gone very well, is demonstrated by a number of random examples from the Dutch metal industry. Thomassen and Drijver-Verblifa, a producer of metal packaging materials, has had great success on the Saudi Arabian soft drinks

Rijnmond ('mouth of the Rhine') region. On the border between industry and farmland.

The concentration of petrochemical industries in the Rijnmond area produces too much air pollution under certain weather conditions. So-called 'sniffing masts' measure the air pollution. If the level of toxins in the air is too great the authorities take measures and alert the population.

market, and produces over a billion cans for that country in one of its plants, that at Oss, which can also manufacture non-standardized formats. A company in the northeast of the country, Nivoba, that has accumulated much experience in the construction of special equipment for the potato starch industry, now also builds starch mills in Africa, Asia, Central and South America, mainly for the cassava (or manioc, yucca), which is very similar to the potato in terms of processing. Klinkenberg/Burosilo, originally (1855) a relatively small company in Wormerveer, started in 1965 with the development of a new type of silo for mass goods. The company has since supplied thirty of these huge warehouses, not only in the Netherlands but also in many foreign countries: West Germany, Austria, Denmark, Turkey and Canada. They have established a branch office in the USA and given licenses to Canada and Japan. Stork Amsterdam B.V. finished building a milk processing plant in Chipinge in Zimbabwe in 1983. It uses imported milk for the local population but can also process milk from Zimbabwe itself and thus stimulates the cattle industry in the area by providing an outlet. Driessen in Limmen, producer of meal carts for the airlines and all kinds of other exchangable aluminium containers for the aviation industry, succeeded in reducing the weight of the carts by thirteen percent. Other improvements were also made. The number of employees has since increased. The firm also has a factory in Wieringerwerf and a sales office in Curaçao. In Apeldoorn there is a construction company specialized in fairground attractions. On the Canadian side of the Niagra Falls, in the 'Maple Leaf Village', is a giant ferris wheel 174 feet high. It is a creation of Bakker-Denies, who are always trying to develop new attractions. The latest is an ingenious mechanism that can move a passenger cabin in several different directions. It is called 'A thousand and one nights' and is very much the center of attention in the always-moving world of the fair. Bakker-Denies has a branch office in Spain that takes care of sales for Southern Europe and Central and South America. The products are remarkable but, since they do not carry a brand name, relatively anonymous. Improvement and inventiveness are the key words here. They work for Bakker-Denies all over the world.

We could easily go on for another few pages, but we will leave it at this: the Netherlands numbers 1500 construction companies and shops in the metal industry. As can be seen from the preceding, the product range is very diversified. It consists further of bridges, flood gates, steel constructions for buildings, offshore installations, of reactors, reservoirs, steam boilers, piping, furthermore of metal furniture, central heating radiators, lighting fixtures, and many additional products. An essential part of the metal products industry is the mass production of bolts, nuts and springs.

The machine industry in the Netherlands is also not restricted to a few products. There are over a thousand companies working in that wide field. Their activities vary from producing office equipment to supplying complete sugar and oil refineries. Apart from tool making machines and other metalworking equipment, machinery is made for the chemical industry, the food and confectionary industry, the wood and furniture industry, the textile industry, paper and graphics enterprises, and for agriculture. Dutch companies have an international clientele for compressors, gas and steam turbines, cooling installations, combustion engines for ships, and electricity plants.

Back to the basics again. In addition to the operations of Hoogovens there is also an independent steel factory with a capacity of about half a million tons of steel per year. Moreover there are various rolling mills, wire drawing mills and pipe factories as well as a large number of iron foundries. In the non-ferro metal sector in the Netherlands there are two aluminium plants and a zinc plant. As for undressed copper, lead and other non-ferro metals, the Netherlands is entirely dependent upon imports. On the other hand, there are the necessary foundries and rolling mills for the processing of these metals.

To end this section a few more specialties. A number of companies have specialized themselves in the casting of ship's propellers, and a number in casting bells and complete bell mechanisms such as carillons or chimes. They can be heard everywhere in the Netherlands and for a long time they formed what passed as the ‘municipal orchestra’ in many towns, where a carillon player often employed by the town produced music on the church bells for all to enjoy. That was the case from about the middle of the seventeenth century when the Hemony brothers greatly improved the art of bell casting. Dutch carillons are now automated but on special occasions are still played by hand, which requires a particular musical skill. The casting is itself also a very specialized skill, and the secret of the craftsmen was only discovered again at the end of the nineteenth century in England.

From church bells to the *chemical industry*. Is it a big step? Not so very big if we go back in history a little, to the time that bell casters also cast cannons, not long after the invention of gunpowder, which for a long time counted as the greatest invention of all time. Gunpowder for a long time made up just about the whole of the ‘chemical industry’ if the production of organic pigments is left aside. How much gunpowder was respected is indicated by the Dutch saying ‘he did not invent gunpowder,’ which means he is

Of the three most famous bell foundries that still operate in Europe today, one is situated in France; the two others are in the Netherlands, one in Aarle Rixtel, the Royal Bell Foundry Petit & Fritsen BV, and the other at Asten, the Royal Eijsbouts B.V., bell foundry and manufacturer of tower clockworks. Both enterprises are known all over the world, not least in the USA, which has formed a particularly large market in recent years. The handwork, the actual casting, is thus a very old craft, but the playing of the carillons can be done in a very modern manner these days, namely by means of computers via an automated mechanism, and also by hand-operated piano keyboards. That does not imply that the classic technique on the so-called lever board has been abandoned. The specialized player of these is still highly respected and is preferred in professional circles to all of the indirect methods.

not very bright. In Europe gunpowder was discovered in the fourteenth century, apparently by accident. Everyone was trying to find an 'alchemical' formula for synthetic gold, and suddenly there was gunpowder, which the Chinese had already known for 1500 years, but had only used for their fireworks. And what had not been thought of during those centuries developed in Europe in a few years: firearms. It took until the eighteenth century until chemistry came up with the possibility to mass produce sulphuric acid. That happened in England around 1760, where it was needed for the bleaching of linen and cotton in the mass production textile mills. Some hundred and fifty years later the textile industry would acquire a whole new look with the rapid popularizing of rayon, the first chemical textile fabric of a long series. Equally unrelated to the textile industry was the production of synthetic dyes which could be made from derivatives of coke and gas production in the time that the blast furnaces became so important. Also aspirin – the first mass produced modern medicine – came, oddly enough, from the same sector. All of the credit here goes to the Germans.

The Netherlands only entered the market very late as a producer of chemical products. But much would be made up in a stroke after the start in 1911 of a small rayon factory that would later become one of the pillars of the large Akzo concern, one of the Netherlands' chemical giants. In 1914 that rayon factory was aleady making a substantial profit. And in the 1920s Enka (later AKU) began to become a world-wide enterprise. It was a genuine chemical industry and the inhabitants of Arnhem and Ede and Hilligersberg could smell it. But many people there brought a fat pay envelope home every week. In the Netherlands there are now more than 300 chemical companies with a total turnover of 10 billion dollars, of which some threequarters come from exports. That is thus very substantial. There are six fertilizer plants, 45 pharmaceutical companies, 15 plastic factories and over 40 companies in the soap, cosmetics and perfume industry. In addition there are manufacturers of paint, lacquer, varnish, dyes, fragrances and flavorings, medicines and dressings, glues, printing inks, synthetic detergents and insecticides. There are nine very large petroleum refineries with a total refining capacity of 85 million tons of crude oil per year. A large share of that capacity is owned by the partly Dutch company Royal/Shell that belongs to one of the biggest companies in the world. The Dutch branch, the Royal, originates entirely from the colonial period and started in 1890 with the oil concession on Sumatra. Originally they were only interested in lamp oil. The well-known sentence 'oil for China's lamps' suggests the extent of the potential sales area. In

A yeast vat (formentor) with a capacity of 26½ thousand gallons at the Gist-Brocades factory in Delft.

Laying of a pipeline at Pernis, Rotterdam.

Installations for the liquefaction of chlorine (foreground) and the condensation of lye (background) of the chemical concern Akzo, Botlek Rotterdam.

Rituals, a novel by Cees Nooteboom, was awarded the Pegasus Prize for Literature in 1982. The Mobil Corporation established this prize and provided for translation into English.

Some other Dutch and Flemish writers who have books available in English are: Anna Blaman (1905-1960), Louis-Paul Boon (1912-1979), Jan Cremer (1940), Frederik van Eeden (1860-1932), Marcellus Emants (1848-1923), Martin Hart (1944), Harry Mulisch (1927), Nescio (1882-1961), Paul van Ostaijen (1896-1928).

There is also an anthology, 'Dutch Interior', with post-war poetry of the Netherlands and Flanders (Columbia University Press, New York).

any case, gasoline was burnt off as a worthless by-product.

In 1897 the English firm Shell was established, which originated from a transport company; as a sideline, it had a trade in shells. The company obtained an oil concession in Borneo. After various forms of cooperation a full merger occurred in 1907. The Royal obtained an interest of 60% in the group, and Shell an interest of 40%. Even before the first world war Royal/Shell had become an enterprise of importance in a large number of countries. In 1918 one of the largest refineries in the world was put into operation in Curaçao. After the second world war that operation was considerably overshadowed by the Shell refinery at Pernis in Rotterdam, the growing port city that would become the biggest oil port in the world. In the middle of the 1970s Shell had 65 refineries all over the world. The assets included more than 300 oil tankers, together with a load capacity of almost 32 million tons. Eleven gas tankers also voyaged on behalf of Shell which could transport a total of more than 25 million cubic feet of natural gas. Pipelines were originally only used for the transport of crude oil, but the rise of natural gas also made it necessary to install giant pipelines for this purpose. By around 1975 Shell possessed no less than 50,000 miles of pipelines (over 20,000 for crude oil, 13,700 for oil products, and over 15,500 for natural gas). With the decreasing importance of petroleum other sectors in Shell have become more important: chemistry, with the emphasis on research, the processing of metals, and the winning and conversion of coal. The company is undergoing a process of restructuring in order to be able to approach the future more forcefully.

Another Dutch giant came into existence at the end of the 1960s: by mergers. We'll have to take a moment for a little history. First the subject of salt. That is present in the Dutch ground in unimaginably large quantities, and in the 1920s and 30s the Royal Dutch Salt Industry (Koninklijke Nederlandsche Zoutindustrie) began to make use of it on a large scale. From that company a large chemical manufacturer would later grow. It incorporated other companies, like a big factory for the production of sulphuric acid and also the pioneering pharmaceutical research and production company Oregon, which had become big from its insulin production. Salt then merged with fibers: AKU, and from that came AKZO.

Another large chemical company is to be found in a corner of the country, in Geleen, where visitors are surprised at the forest of piping and equipment situated so far from the big centers. Here thousands of miners used to work but the mines are now closed. What remained, and continues in full glory, is the chemical company of the State mines (DSM) that has three possibilities for transport: road, rail and the Juliana canal.

In the center of the country we finally find the Chemische Fabriek Naarden that grew into a multinational enterprise.

Then the sector of plastics processing must also be mentioned. The application of synthetics is continuously increasing. The automobile alone is good proof of that; each year more parts are replaced by synthetic materials. In the Netherlands more than 250 companies are active in this sector. Annual turnover is about one billion dollars, of which about a third comes from exports. Of those, 50 thousand tons is synthetic rubber used in conveyor belts, car tires and in all kinds of medical goods.

The most important export sector is electrical and electronics apparatus. The best known *electronics* company is Philips, long established in Eindhoven, once a sleepy town in the south of North Brabant province. Today it is the fifth largest city in the Netherlands, with about 200,000 inhabitants. Visitors to this city with its modern center – it was rebuilt after the war – must not miss the Evoluon building. It is a permanent Philips exposition that shows the staggering development of science and technology, but also an electronic playground for children.

Philips started in the last century as a manufacturer of light bulbs. Through the development of radio tubes the company moved into the mass production of radio sets, with which it began expanding just before the Depression (1929). At that time Philips employed an unprecedented 26,000 people in Eindhoven. The economic crisis led not only to many dismissals but also to the erection of tariff barriers throughout the world. Instead of succumbing to these, Philips actually continued to expand, by setting up foreign companies wherever it could. Since that time the company has always found strength in difficult circumstances. An example. As a manufacturer of light bulbs Philips was interested in bicycle lamps, an article much in demand in bicycle-conscious Holland. At Philips a generator for bikes was also tried. The marketing of this product was not very successful. The basic apparatus was then rebuilt as an electric shaver. This was a great success. And it still is, throughout the entire world. From that time household equipment became ever more important. In the meantime, particularly after the second world war, a process of nationalization was set forth. Partly as a result a new shift occurred: from consumer goods to professional equipment and accessories. That meant an expansion of customers; from individual consumers to large enterprises and even – more and more often – governments at home and abroad. Because a national government prefers to do business with its own industries this stimulated Philips to localize the most advanced parts of its production in as many countries as possible. Working with governments is nothing new to Philips. For many years

Insight Holland

Philips has enjoyed a position of power economically as a mass employer and mass exporter. That was why the government allowed Philips to use the Netherlands experimentally for the gradual introduction of television. That was, in the 1950s – just as now – a matter of necessity for Philips. The influence of this company on the composition of the first governments after the second world war was unmistakable. If the planned wage policy had a socialistic side, then it also certainly had a capitalistic purpose.

Aside from Philips there are another 250 companies in the Netherlands engaged in the electronics sector. Together they have a turnover of about $ 5.5 billion, of which about 65% is obtained from exports. The Dutch electronics industry as a whole can supply any article imaginable in this field. Many important innovations are from the Netherlands. Philips is at the top with inventions requiring a great deal of research investment. The tape cassette, the laser video disc, and the audio compact disc are only a few examples. Philips is an unmissable part of the picture of the technical evolution in the world.

Whoever travels through the Netherlands will see a picture of great activity everywhere. One can also watch it while seated: in the restaurant that has been built over the main highway from Amsterdam to The Hague and Rotterdam, one is looking at one of the busiest roadways of Western Europe. In the air much activity can also be seen. Nearby is Schiphol, the airport of Amsterdam, of the entire Netherlands and of a large part of Western Europe. Schiphol is very important as a transfer and transit port. The traffic on the roads and in the air leave no doubt: The Netherlands is a *transport country*. Is it also a country with a transporter industry? A glance in the air reveals many Fokkers, an old aircraft name from even before the first world war. Since 1945 in particular Fokker has had some notable successes, such as the turboprop F 28, of which more than 200 have left the factory. At the same time, the Dutch aircraft industry, working with other industries and scientific institutes, is engaged in the space industry. The first Dutch astronomical satellite (ANS) was a complete success. Another to which the Dutch contributed was designed to measure infrared radiation in space. Satellites of various kinds are becoming increasingly important and the manufacture of them requires much research and many skilled workers. A whole new future is present here.

What transport means for the Netherlands can also be further discovered on the entirely man-made peninsula of the Maasvlakte. Here, in the New Waterway, can be seen the busiest shipping traffic in the world. There are seagoing tugs, passenger ships, submarines, aircraft carriers, yachts, even merchant vessels with

Around the greatest harbor in the world, Rotterdam, the building and repair of ships has always been an important activity.

Repair of a drilling platform in a drydock in Rotterdam.

The Dutch firm DAF (Van Doorne's Automobile Factory) stems from a small machine manufacturer (1928) which changed its name in 1934 to Van Doorne's trailer factory. Trailers, truck trailers, and off-the-road vehicles for military and civil use were manufactured. In 1950 a factory for cars was established, and eight years later a small passenger car with automatic transmission appeared on the market: the DAF. For a long time this was a very common sight in Dutch traffic. At the end of 1972 a cooperative agreement was reached with the Swedish company Volvo, and also the American International Harvester Company. It has already been many years since DAF cars ceased to be made, but the name DAF still stands proudly on the many commercial vehicles that leave the factory in Eindhoven.

names from all countries, and coasters, and tankers. One can see floating docks, cranes, pipe-laying ships and even complete drilling platforms. Much of all that floating iron can be produced by the Netherlands itself in a substantial number of shipbuilding wharves, a few of which were founded more than a century ago. They became great with the development of the steamship, and with the growth during the last century in world trade. Under the pressure of the times there has been a continuous increasing specialization in particular types of vessels, such as the refrigerated ship, the hydrofoil, the pipe-laying ship, the self-loading dredger, oil platforms.

Also worthwhile for those struggling to gain a picture of the modern Netherlands is a visit to the terrain of the Floriade, an exhibition park of flowers and plants in Amsterdam, especially of the art of cultivation and horticulture. In the parking lot many a Volvo will be seen that has been manufactured in the Netherlands by a company that once started as a construction workshop for trailers and containers. And that became very big, also as a supplier to the military. Also other companies in that sector have grown. In the lovely park terrain, among all those Dutch flowers and plants, is a symbol that connects the history of the country with its future, a modern windmill. It is the wind turbine Pioneer 1. Its rotor spins around a vertical shaft, has a diameter of about fifty feet and can supply 100 kilowatts of power; this goes to the municipal electricity company. The rotor has been designed by Fokker, the famous aircraft company, but manufactured by the small Plymarin in Medemblik. This Pioneer 1 therefore serves as a symbol of the Netherlands because it makes use of an old form of energy. And because it is characteristic of the fact that the Netherlands is not standing still – that it continues its pioneering ways in big as well as small companies.

133

Why don't you come again?

Let's just say that the Netherlands is a very special place.

Insight Holland

The Netherlands is a country with many advantages, especially for the tourist. And with only a few disadvantages. The main disadvantage is that the Netherlands has too much of everything. It is hard to believe how many possibilities there are for things to see and do in this small land. And there are so many different ways of seeing the sights.

It does not even matter in which of the eleven provinces one stays. Everywhere the visitor will find a great wealth of attractions. People who are interested in art will not find such a rich diversity in such a small area anywhere else in the world – from ancient art to very modern. Families with children will discover the nicest recreation parks everywhere. Those with a technical interest can find, in the north and the west, in the south and the east, staggering examples of engineering technique and modern enterprise. Visitors with an agricultural interest will discover public institutions which can inform them in the most lively manner about agriculture, stock-breeding and horticulture in the Low Countries. For other vacationers there are the dunes, the beautiful beaches of the North Sea, the many lakes to sail on and there is also the large body of water of the former Southern Sea. Everywhere one can make lovely tours on hired bikes. And always the visitor will discover that every attraction, every museum, every event is unique. He experiences something indefinable that ultimately can only be captured in one word: *Holland*. It is a feeling, especially a paradoxical feeling, caused by that small scale, the greatness of ideas and daring, the vulnerability and the impressiveness of the many ways in which the country has outgrown itself. Let's just say that the Netherlands is a very special place. So why don't you come? In the Netherlands you will experience the peculiar sensation of immediately feeling at home in surroundings which are yet very uncommon. Even people who have already read or heard a lot about the country, even those who lived there when they were young, will not experience the country as just a country. Right away they will get in touch with the surprising part of the Netherlands. The specialness of the vast skies, the green meadows, the compact city centers and the fact that everything is situated so nearby. Everything is familiar, homelike. After a few hours many people get the feeling of having dreamed about the country. From pictures of course, television broadcasts. But stronger. Usually this does not apply to visitors of Dutch origin, people who left the country some time ago. They are so overwhelmed by all the changes of the last thirty-five years during the first hours that they only recognize their old country here and there, by grassy green bits and water blue pieces. But what everybody experiences and many will re-experience is the atmosphere of hospitality. Everybody feels welcome because the Dutch are ready to answer any questions. Not only in Dutch, but almost just as well in English. Or in German. And a little less well, but understandable, in French. The Netherlands has become a very international country without losing its own identity.

There is something else that will quickly help the visitor to feel at ease. That is the public transport system. In the centers of cities with a large population there are – aside from taxicabs – fast buses and streetcars and in a few places urban trains – metros – that can take you to all the important places. Also right to the train stations, which still play a major role in Dutch city life. The public system of buses, metros, streetcars, trains and even ferry boats – which still operate here and there – has been harmonized into one organization. In all parts of the country one can buy the same 'strippen' card which is valid for all public transport everywhere. Any conductor can immediately explain how it works or otherwise the man in the tobacco shop, where these cards are also sometimes sold.

The best source of information upon arrival about hotels, restaurants, organized excursions, is the official tourist office that you will recognize by the letters VVV, which stand for *Vereniging voor Vreemdelingenverkeer*, in English something like Association for Tourist Traffic. In every big city you will find a VVV office with qualified personnel who know the answers to practically any questions. Also in smaller towns, and sometimes even in villages, you will encounter the letters VVV.

If you intend to travel through the Netherlands or even through the whole of Europe the ANWB is also of great importance to you. The letters stand for the Royal Netherlands Touring Club and this

Madurodam between The Hague and Scheveningen, where many noteworthy Dutch structures can be seen in miniature.

Since 1903 the royal family has made use of the Golden Coach for special occasions, such as the annual ceremonial opening of the States-General (Parliament). Drawn by eight horses the State Coach travels at walking pace through The Hague. The coach is richly decorated with allegorical images and is of course not of gold, but is entirely gilded.

organization can be compared to those such as the AAA in the United States. Members of the AAA can also receive the full services of the ANWB on their membership cards: maps, route suggestions, etc. Those who are not already automatically entitled to membership benefits through such reciprocal arrangements can join for not too much money.

Because transportation is so easy and fast in the Netherlands it does not really matter which big city you choose to stay in. Rotterdam is favorably situated for visitors to some sights such as the *Delta works*. The Hague is for people who want to also enjoy the sea and going out in Scheveningen. Amsterdam has the advantage of a central location. But, as already pointed out, there are frequent train connections between the cities. With a car one can also travel rapidly between these cities as the roads – all freeways – are excellent.

If you want to become acquainted with all of the Netherlands in a rapid and well-ordered way, then you should in fact go first to The Hague. There the Dutch have made an entertaining joke of their small land by making it even smaller – namely in the miniature city of *Madurodam*. It has been built on a scale of 25:1, so each step you make there counts for 25 in the Netherlands itself. You will feel like a giant there, a Gulliver in Lilliput, and the sensation is much the same, because everything there lives and moves, ships in the harbor, traffic on the four-lane highway. You will find there most of the important structures of the Netherlands brought together: Schiphol Airport, the railway system, windmills, and a lot of canal houses. All together one hundred and fifty of the country's most famous buildings, including the Frans Hals Museum of Haarlem. In the summer it is also open in the evenings and then you can enjoy Madurodam – the city 'Holland' – brightly illuminated by 50,000 tiny street lamps.

Ideally you should time your visit to Madurodam for the third Monday of September and then spend the night in The Hague, because on the third Tuesday of September the royal procession of 'Prinsjesdag' traditionally takes place. Then you can see Beatrix, Queen of the Netherlands, ride in her golden coach from the Palace to the center of government, the Throne Room at the Binnenhof. There she presents the Speech from the Throne, the annual address to the nation spelling out government policy for the coming year. There is also something of a fairytale atmosphere here, just as at Madurodam, for however businesslike the Dutch may be in their approach to industry or agriculture, and however oriented they may be to the future, there is so much history in this country and so many links to it that a certain air of unreality also seems to permeate some aspects of the Dutch national consciousness.

The country is filled with splendid *museums*; it would be impossible to give an overview of all of these. Amsterdam has some of the biggest and most famous ones, more or less coincidentally sited conveniently close to each other near the equally famous *Concertgebouw* where – especially at the beginning of this century – musical history has been made. Music lovers should not miss an afternoon or evening concert here. Amsterdam is in every respect an extraordinary city with a flourishing and relaxed cultural life. In the area of the Leidseplein alone, a lively square that with its surrounding streets forms one of the city's nightlife centers, you will find at least fifty cafés, restaurants, discotheques and snack bars and nearly each one will have its own distinctive characteristic atmosphere. That also applies to many cafés in Rotterdam, The Hague, Arnhem, Groningen, Maastricht, whichever big town you choose.

'Gezellig' which means 'nice atmosphere' is a very Dutch expression. The Dutch enjoy a feeling of intimacy together, whether at home or in the café. The center of Rotterdam – one of the busiest ports in the world – was rebuilt after the bombardment of 1940 as a modern business district where Americans in particular quickly feel at home, especially on the *Lijnbaan*, a large, luxurious shopping precinct. The Hague on the other hand has kept its *Passage*, a high-roofed shopping gallery of iron and glass retaining the atmosphere of the last century. Here one finds the spirit of the Crystal Palace and similar edifices. For people who are interested in cities, urban planning and urban renewal in particular, Utrecht's *Hoog-Catharijne* is a sight to see. Utrecht, a main railway junction, began choking on its obsolete, nineteenth century inner city quarters after the war. The railway station was integrated into a new city plan and the great work was carried out in the 1960s and 70s by the construction company Bredero. It is now possible in Utrecht to spend an entire day shopping, eating out, and going out in the evening without once exposing oneself to the elements. Adjoining the big complex of glass and concrete is the old inner town with its medieval canals and quiet little squares. The shopkeepers in this part have also been carried forward by the prosperity of the new.

The mixture of old and new and the interchange between them is something typical of the Netherlands. In one or two days you can experience this for yourself by making a tour around the former Southern Sea, now called the *IJsselmeer*, to the river IJssel, a side branch of the Rhine. It is best to start in Amsterdam. You can choose an organized bus tour – not the worst method – but you can also go on your own, by car or even by bicycle if you adjust

The Concertgebouw orchestra *during a performance in the main hall of the* Concertgebouw *in Amsterdam, Christmas 1983.*

138

the route to your own physical capabilities.

You travel through an old, still perfect polderland in a northerly direction to the old fishing towns of Volendam, on the mainland, and to Marken, which is no longer a real island since there is now a connecting dike. In both towns folkloristic costumes are still commonly worn (mainly for the tourists). You can get a clear picture though of how the fishermen and farmers live there along the old inland sea two, three, four hundred years ago. You can also see this magnificently in the two-fold Zuiderzee Museum in Enkhuizen. In the open-air museum – a complete village – authentic houses, work places and cafés have been brought together. In the indoor museum, in the town itself eight minutes' walk away, the exhibition includes a splendid collection of sailing vessels.

Not far from Enkhuizen begins the nearly twenty miles of the *Af-*

In the many excellent sandwich shops, or 'broodjeswinkels' in the big cities, every visitor can discover what the Dutch like to eat. On display are the large assortment of fillings to be had on rolls, such as 'halfom' or the juicy Dutch roast beef, as well as all kinds of cheese. A visit to such a sandwich shop is an excellent way to make a first acquaintance with the Netherlands. Especially do not forget to order a Dutch specialty: meat or shrimp croquette. This is a deep-fried ragout pastry, crisp on the outside, soft and glowing hot on the inside.

HUSSAR SALAD

According to tradition Hussar salad is a dish made of left-overs which owes its name to the faithful cavalry soldiers who, in the distant past of the live-in servant girl, would secretly visit his true love in the kitchen in the evening. The besotted girl would see what was left over and quickly prepare a tasty snack for her lover. There were as many versions as there were servant girls. Here is the so-called light Hussar salad (four people).

7 ounces of cold meat, preferably veal
1 cooked beet
8 cold boiled potatoes
2 slightly sour apples
pickled onions and gherkins
mayonnaise
bouillon or gravy
1 hard-boiled egg

Cut the meat in small pieces and the potatoes in small blocks. Grate a small onion, chop two slightly sour apples, do the same with a large dill pickle, and if desired, a couple of pickled onions. Mix everything together lightly and add in oil and vinegar as well as a touch of mustard, salt, pepper, and perhaps some bouillon or – better still – real gravy. Finally a bit of mayonnaise can be added. Give it a pleasing form, spread mayonnaise over it, and garnish the salad with slices of egg, pickle and some cooked red beet.

sluitdijk, on which a four-lane highway and a cycling path have been laid, and that is also very Dutch. At the Monument, where the dike was closed in 1932, there is a possibility to have something to eat or drink or to climb the dike. To the north you will then see the Wadden Sea and perhaps a suggestion of the Wadden Islands beyond the horizon. And to the south you will have a view over the vast surface of Lake IJssel: once salt water, now sweet, the fishing area of many eel fishermen.

When you have crossed the Afsluitdijk you should go south. You will find the village of Makkum, where you are welcome in a very old pottery dating from 1660. The company is now in the hands of the ninth generation of the founding family! If you are lucky, you will be personally guided around the premises by Mr. Tichelaar, and that name means, really, tile maker.

A little bigger than tiny Makkum is the next interesting village: Hindelopen, where the tradition of a characteristic decorative art reigns. There is also a museum: the Hidde Nijland foundation. If you want to buy something you won't have any trouble finding shops for it.

At the harbor town of Lemmer we enter the *Noordoostpolder*, the land created by the Dutch themselves, which became dry in 1942, in the middle of the war. Emmeloord is the capital, an 'historic' example of urban planning. Drive from here to the old island of Urk, which is now part of the mainland but whose inhabitants still maintain their religion and culture in some isolation – very strictly. You are welcome, but not particularly on a Sunday, the day of the Lord. In any case you had better not cycle through the village on that day. Walking is okay, but be modest.

Continuing, we cross the Ketel bridge to the two newest polders, which together form a single whole: Flevoland (eastern and southern). Take a look at how much land the Dutch have won back from their old enemy, and friend, the sea. Here space to live and work has been created, 'Lebensraum', but then in a very peaceful manner. In order to get an impression of what it was originally all about in these new polders, you should go to the new village of Biddinghuizen, where the National Agricultural Exhibition can be found in the *Flevohof*. There you can get a good impression of how far the Dutch have progressed in their animal husbandry (cows, pigs and chickens in abundance), their horticulture and in the art of growing flowers. Among many other things – because there is much, much more – you can see how cheese is made: from the feeding of the cows to the milking, the curdling of the milk and the aging of the cheese.

Now go to Lelystad and see how the old ideas have changed under the pressure of new times, and how agriculture – though not all of it – is being pushed aside by urban development on a large scale. The modern residential community of Lelystad is splendidly centrally located. Soon it will be linked by train via Amsterdam to Schiphol Airport, and further to The Hague and Rotterdam. A rail line to the northeast of the country is on the drawing boards. The increasing activity of the industrial area is already anticipating this. If you drive to the southwest on the outer dike, you will see to your left a rich nature preserve, a breeding place for thousands of birds. It is kept in a state as natural as possible and in this way the organized Netherlands has gained another beautiful wilderness area.

There are also areas for pure recreation in this polder. They were included in the original blueprints to make leisure activities more meaningful through an integration with nature.

Finally, not far from where you leave the two interlinked polders, you will arrive in the large, obviously still growing urban conglomerate of *Almere* and Almere harbor, which together form a satellite town of the capital Amsterdam. This large chunk of urbanization will in time come to develop its own identity, but it was intended in the first place to give some breathing space, both indoors and out, to refugees from the overcrowded Randstad area.

What did we want to achieve with this tour around and across the bottom of the old Southern Sea? We wanted to give you one example. We could easily have chosen ten other routes. We could have told you about cathedrals and churches. Markets and unusual old buildings. About the open-air museum in Arnhem. About port towns in Zeeland. Boat excursions. About the flower auction in Aalsmeer. About the big floral exhibition called Keukenhof. About the Wadden islands. About castles everywhere: a hundred and fifty! Ninety-nine percent we have not told. When you have visited the Netherlands and returned home, and your neighbor asks if you have seen 'this and that', then you may say: 'No, I missed that, but I saw that and this.' Because that is the marvellous thing about the Netherlands: You can cross it in a day. But you cannot see all of it in a lifetime.

Castle De Haar in Haarzuilens, near Utrecht, built in the 12th century. Completely restored at the end of the last century and now partly a museum with a lovely collection of tapestries, old furniture and ceramics.

PHOTO CREDITS

Openbaar Lichaam Rijnmond, Rotterdam: 127 (bottom)
–: Tom van Oosterhout: 127 (top)
PGEM, Arnhem: 130 (top)
Philips, Eindhoven: 14 (top), 39 (left), 131
Provinciale Bibliotheek Zeeland, Middelburg: 46, 47
Ridder, de, Amsterdam: 68
Rijks Instituut voor Oorlogsdocumentatie, Amsterdam: 40
Rijksmuseum, Amsterdam: 56
Rijkspolitie, Apeldoorn: 116
Rijksvoorlichtingsdienst, 's-Gravenhage: 14, 15
Rijkswaterstaat, deltadienst, Zierikzee: 13, 104, 105
Rijkswaterstaat, directie Zuiderzeewerken, Lelystad: 37 (bottom), 101,
    102
Scheepvaartmuseum, Amsterdam: 30
Singer, Amsterdam: 65
Stadsreiniging, Amsterdam: 72 (top)
Stichting Public Relations Land- en Tuinbouw, 's-Gravenhage: 6, 7, 71,
    110, 111 (left), 112 (bottom), 113, 117, 120, 121, 122
Van Nelle-Lassie, Rotterdam, 125
Veer, Kees van der, Euro-Book Productions, Amsterdam: 90, 93
Vereniging voor Bitumineüze Werken, Breukelen: 38, 97, 103
Verkade, Zaandam: 62
Verolme Botlek, Rozenburg: 132 (bottom)
Volker Stevin, Rotterdam: 99
Volvo Cars, Born: 133 (top)
Vries-Metz, W. de, Amsterdam: 8, 141
Wereldcontact, Zeist: 54

© 1983 *text*: Max Dendermonde, Sarasota (USA)
© 1984 *English edition*: Kosmos bv, Utrecht/ Antwerp

Translation from the Dutch by Carla van Rijsbergen, Amsterdam

Cover: illustration by Kees van der Veer, as poster available from Euro-Book Productions, Amsterdam
Bookdesign: Karel van Laar, De Bilt
Illustration research: Hermien Dijkstra, Amsterdam

D/1984/0108/430

CIP-GEGEVENS

Dendermonde, Max

Insight Holland / Max Dendermonde; [transl. from the Dutch by Carla van Rijsbergen]. – Utrecht [etc.]:
Kosmos. – Ill.
ISBN 90-215-1221-1
SISO 982   UDC 914.92   UGI 610
Trefw.: Nederland; reisgidsen.